10649306

CROSSFIRE

CROSSFIRE
A Litany for Survival

POEMS 1998–2019

Staceyann Chin

Foreword by Jacqueline Woodson

Haymarket Books
Chicago, Illinois

© 2019 Staceyann Chin

Published in 2019 by
Haymarket Books
P.O. Box 180165
Chicago, IL 60618
773-583-7884
www.haymarketbooks.org
info@haymarketbooks.org

ISBN: 978-1-64259-025-8

Distributed to the trade in the US through Consortium Book Sales and
Distribution (www.cbsd.com) and internationally through Ingram Publisher
Services International (www.ingramcontent.com).

This book was published with the generous support of Lannan Foundation
and Wallace Action Fund.

Cover photograph by Julia Pearl Robbins. Cover design by Brett Neiman.

Library of Congress Cataloging-in-Publication data is available.

Printed in Canada by union labor.

10 9 8 7 6 5 4 3 2 1

For Hazel and Zuri-Siale
who bookend my survival

For those of us
who were imprinted with fear

...

And when the sun rises we are afraid
it might not remain
when the sun sets we are afraid
it might not rise in the morning
when our stomachs are full we are afraid
of indigestion
when our stomachs are empty we are afraid
we may never eat again
when we are loved we are afraid
love will vanish
when we are alone we are afraid
love will never return
and when we speak we are afraid
our words will not be heard
nor welcomed
but when we are silent
we are still afraid

So it is better to speak
remembering
we were never meant to survive.

from "A Litany for Survival" by Audre Lorde

CONTENTS

FOREWORD

Jacqueline Woodson

Step into the crossfire.

This is a world you know everything about, because in Staceyann's hands the minutiae of our everyday lives becomes a love song to anyone who has ever had to live a life.

Step into the crossfire.

This is a world you know nothing about, because in Chin's hands, this love song to survival is her own crossfire of motherhood and love and hurt and pain and race and survival coming fast, coming hard, coming at her with intention and ferocity.

With her brilliant hands, she has crafted this crossfire into a lullaby we all need to hear. A song that points us each toward the tools we must gather for our own daily survival.

Step into the crossfire.

Ride the A-train and Amtrak. Move to America from Jamaica. Lose a mother. Give birth to a daughter. Remember that:

You are only human. A frail light among many lights

Step into this stunning world.

And be forever changed.

PREFACE

Staceyann Chin

Many of these poems have been alive for more than two decades. They have begun in my journals, in my mouth, and then graduated to audiences in countless countries, where they have lived on numerous stages. They have been bellowed, whispered, edited, re-edited, discarded, retrieved, rejected—some have been posted online, a few have been included in anthologies, journals, and media publications, but never in a collection of poems authored by me.

It's taken me years to decipher why I have never published a collection of poems. In the early years, after Def Poetry Jam on Broadway and on HBO—which, incidentally, feels like it happened only a few minutes after I landed in the US—there were many offers to publish the poems that had, for all intents and purposes, erupted from what felt like a self-imposed exile from my home. But I'm Caribbean—a Jamaican girl educated at the University of the West Indies, in the revered tradition of the postcolonial—so I thought any poem I wrote, the mere mewling of a young, unseasoned writer. But people kept asking for the poems, so in the performance tradition of the 1990s, I made a compromise and self-published chapbooks. I hawked those at my readings for a few years, then stopped. They didn't feel like real books: bound, attached to a press, with an ISBN number. I wanted to be a real writer, but I couldn't bring myself to think myself a real poet, like Derek Walcott. I felt I had to wait until I was at least thirty. Thirty sounded more appropriate, more weighted, more like someone who had lived enough to write about it—someone who could handle the task of metaphors and similes and meter and rhyme with depth and pathos.

The more well-known I became, the more glaring the missing collection seemed. For years, I sent blocks of poems to professors who were teaching my work. Many of them became adept at transcribing the text from the plethora of performances posted on YouTube and other places online.

The year I met Derek Walcott, I was still young. I made a joke about the way St. Lucians pronounce the word "chicken," and we both collapsed into a shared mirth that excluded the Americans in the room. We talked about two of my old professors—contemporaries of his—Mervyn Morris and Edward Baugh. We talked about being caught between the cultural worlds of the United States and the Caribbean. We bonded over the dexterity required to pronounce and spell English words correctly while in each location. He took a shine to me, I suppose, and invited me to study with him, to audit his class at Boston University. I went for three days a week for six months. I sat in his class with maybe ten other students, and read T. S. Eliot, W. H. Auden, and Seamus Heaney. We discussed what makes a poem good and what makes it operatic. I learned a lot about poetry from being in Walcott's class that year. But something about the interaction bothered me.

Every day, after each class, he'd invite me to lunch with him. I wasn't a regular student on campus, so I was grateful for the company. And he was very funny; he told a lot of stories about his life as a poet. I learned that he had started publishing at a very early age. His mother gave him the money to publish his first book of poems. His pen was immediately loved and accepted by those in power. He had a burning desire to write, and those around him respected his drive. He was always seen as a golden child, and he was fairly comfortable with seeing himself as such. I never had that. My work was despised by many. Ridiculed by some. Mostly sensationalized in the Caribbean press. Every time I went home to read, there were numerous articles, ad nauseam, which discussed my sexuality as deviance, something I picked up in the amoral culture of the American North. No one ever talked about my worth as a writer. It was always lesbian this and Jesus that and questions about how Jamaican I could be with my homosexuality so prevalent in my narrative.

Walcott was mostly kind to me. He would often say that I too had the gift of the pen, that I could turn a good phrase, that my race politics were promising, that my poems had a precision of language that pulled the reader in—that was all good and well, he maintained, but I had to stop writing all this feminist foolishness. Nobody would care about sexual orientation and my vagina or its basic bodily functions a hundred years from now, he said. I was, of course, deeply flattered by his praise of my use of language, but greatly disturbed by his dismissive notes on the very core of my reason for writing. I didn't know how to write without centering my politics, my identity as a lesbian and a woman, my female body, and how it made me vulnerable in a world dictated by the desires and rules of cisgender men.

Without knowing it, my time with Walcott further cemented the feeling that I was a poet who had the potential to be a good poet, but that I wasn't there yet. The poems continued to live, dynamic on stages, but dormant on my various hard drives. I made a good living performing. So I never worried about being relevant, about lasting.

Plus, I had already published a relatively successful memoir about growing up in Jamaica. The publication of *The Other Side of Paradise* made me a "published author" and gave me room to NOT address the issue of the unpublished poems.

In the ten years between then and the collection in question, *Crossfire*, I've met plenty of other writers I respect who had warm words for my work. I met Walter Mosley shortly after my time with Walcott. Generous and supportive, he immediately compared me to Sonia Sanchez and Ntozake Shange, and to Shakespeare, whose poems lived in rooms of people who were electrified and shaken by the works of those writers being read aloud. Walter introduced me to Edwidge Danticat—who in my opinion is the final authority on important work. Danticat looked me in the eye and told me my work was important and brave and necessary. Even the pieces about my body and its female functions. For ten years I existed in a state of poetic purgatory; a fairly large, live, eager audience, but almost no readers of the work I fretted about, for draft after draft, to put on the page before reading it out loud to anyone.

Then I had a baby and crossed over the forty mark. I immediately began obsessing about death and permanence and legacy and heritage. As a new mother, I also had far less time to be emailing reams of poems to professors who wanted to teach my work. The question of a collection of poems became more urgent with every passing birthday.

Walcott passed. Ntozake Shange passed. All of a sudden, it felt ridiculous to have avoided publishing. I felt quite foolish and a bit naive. Here I was, forty-six years old, a fairly known poet for twenty of those years, and not one volume of poetry to show for it.

In walks Anthony Arnove, who didn't hesitate when I suggested Haymarket as a home for this odd first/collected book of poems, so desperately in need of a resting place. I had worked with Anthony long enough on Howard Zinn's *Voices of a People's History of the United States*, to know he would be a good partner on this very unorthodox journey for these never-published poems, which spanned the gamut from poems written in my early twenties to poems written this year, to poems edited for performance, to poems with little performative value at all. Maya Marshall, my trusty editor, has been the kind of stealthy a poet who has lived with and performed her own work for decades needs. She's asked more questions than she's given directives, and was always so patient as I avoided her queries and buried my head in the sand of these muddled pages. I am very grateful I had her quiet guidance to reach for when I needed, and her ready silence when I required it.

If I'm being completely candid, I wish I had published volumes at different points in the life I see in my rear view, volumes that might speak more specifically about each chapter of that life. Plus, it's ageist to think that only older people have valuable thoughts to add to the canon of writing about the human condition. Time certainly provides perspective, but that perspective often comes at the expense of the one you are having in the moment. It would be illuminating to read today what the writer in me at twenty-five would have deemed important, what I would have chosen to publish at thirty-five. As it stands now, this will be a giant soup into which we have thrown everything, including the proverbial kitchen sink.

These poems are a map of my life. They tell the story of parents who had cause to leave me, the people who were forced to step in—both willingly and unwillingly—the politics that have shaped me, how those politics have evolved with time and experience, the failures from which I've learned, the many lovers I have survived, the ones who barely survived me. It chronicles the birth of my daughter, my life with my grandmother, the distance from my brother, the convoluted journey with my mother, and much, much more. Reading through this volume makes me sad and happy and hopeful and proud and waiting with baited breath, in anticipation of the lives I have yet to live.

CROSSFIRE

CROSSFIRE

Am I a feminist
or a womanist
the student needs to know
if I do men occasionally
and primarily am I a lesbian

tongue tied up in my cheek
I attempt to respond with some honesty—

this business of dykes and dykery I tell her
is often messy
with social tensions as they are
you never quite know what you're getting
—girls who are only straight at night
—hardcore butches be sporting dresses
between nine and six during the day
          sometimes he is a she
trapped by the limitations of our imagination

primarily I tell her
I am concerned about young women
who are raped on college campuses
          in cars
after poetry readings like this one
          in bars
          bruised lip and broken heart
you will forgive her if she does not come
forward with the truth immediately
for when she does it is she who will stand trial
as damaged goods

everyone will say she asked for it
dressed as she was she must have wanted it

the words will knock about in her head
horny bitch
slut/tease
harlot
loose woman
some people cannot handle a woman on the loose

you know those women in silk ties and pin-striped shirts
those women in blood-red stilettos and short pink skirts
these women make New York City the most colorful place
    and while we're on the subject of diversity
    Asia is not one big race
    and there is no such country called the *Islands*
    and no—I am not from there

there are a hundred ways to slip between the cracks
of our not-so-credible cultural assumptions of race and religion

most people are surprised my father is Chinese—like
there's some kind of preconditioned
look for the half-Chinese/lesbian/poet
who used to be Catholic but now believes in dreams

let's keep it real
says the boy in the double-X hooded sweatshirt
that blond haired/blue eyed/Jesus in the Vatican ain't right
    that motherfucker was Jewish, not white

Christ was a Middle Eastern Rastaman
who ate grapes in the company of prostitutes
and drank wine more than he drank water
born of the spirit the disciples also loved him in the flesh
but the discourse is on people who clearly identify as gay
or lesbian or straight
the State needs us to be left or right
    those in the middle get caught
in the cross/fire away at the other side

if you are not for us you must be against us
  (people get scared
  enough they pick a team)

but be it for Buddha or for Krishna or for Christ
God is that place between belief and what you name it
I believe holy is what you do
when there is nothing between your actions and a truth
  never one thing or the other—
I am everything I fear
  tears and sorrows
  black windows and muffled screams
in the morning I am all I ever wanted to be
  rain and laughter
  bare footprints and invisible seams
always without breath or definition—I claim every single dawn
for yesterday is simply what I was
and tomorrow
even that will be gone

COMMON TRUTHS, OR:
WHY I LOVE MY PUSSY

Women have always been
the center of things beautiful for me
becoming woman
has always been the center of my girlhood

the sum of my thighs
ankles
even my shoulders were always girl

when I bled for the first time
I told my best friend

wrapped my secret in her ear
and assured her
that this blood meant we could make babies

       but being girl in Jamaica
in 1980 meant I had to run faster
than my cousin's fingers/farther
than his sweaty palms reaching for my hands
my tiny breasts had to be brave
against his fury when I refused

one night I stabbed him
pencil point sliding swift into his flesh
the whole house cried out
and I was proud of my yellow pencil
point sharp and without fear

my aunt beat me anyways
for making your cousin bleed, she said
and I cried more out of loneliness
than anything

the other cousin's name
still remains quiet upon my tongue

I think of him
when I am sad or angry
or afraid of things that do not make noises in the dark

stark raving mad
he showed me his dick
told me *you smell like a woman*
in that little girl's body
hips barely budding he cornered me

in the hallway
the bathroom

when I bled
I washed quick and quiet

years later he still smiles at me
even now
no apologies necessary
I was only a girl

quick and quiet girls learn
to wash the details away
bury them under briefs

jeans
cargo pants

under these panties
rests the story of these chochas
these twats/these bushes that bleed

on time
once a month I am reminded
that though I have not yet given birth

I can
my pussy can do something
no dick or tomcat can

I dare you to make people
without a vagina

Shiva
or man
or beast
even Jesus had to pass through a punani

        angels and messengers aside
Mary had to lend passage to God
or them Christians might still be Jews

waiting for a Christ
that was stuck up the ass of some man
who thought he could
do what even little girls are forced to do
in Sri Lanka
in Uganda
in South Carolina

everyday
against our wishes
we carry common stories of sons
and fathers
and cousins who violate the sanctity of these bodies

these breasts
this ability to make breath
from passion
or the neat decision of an intent

one day
I hope my belly will bloom little miracles called Andrea

or Elisha
or Alexander

mouths will open wide
in wonder
and terror
everyday men ponder
the magic of what vaginas do
everyday
women carry people into being

and everyday
even on the most petrifying day
I stand grateful I was born
bloody snatch in just the right place
today I am glad I am a girl

       especially since yesterday
my mother told me
go ahead and write your story

no matter that I will write her
in unflattering truths
write
she told me
and I hope the book sells
so you can afford to raise a daughter
with a heart like yours

and everything was better
between us

it did not matter that she left me
twice
no matter that in Jamaica
in 1972
in 1980

she chose her safety over mine

yesterday
she said *write/my daughter*
and the world righted itself

I wish
that every mother whose daughter
survived the burial of unspoken things
would give her permission
to say what happened

to *write* down how she endured
the terror of being a small girl
in a world that so deeply favors men

I wish every cunt had the courage
to bear public witness
I wish every woman
had a pen, a clear view, and the support
she needs to scream:
what happened to me was not my fault
what happened to me was not my fault
WHAT HAPPENED TO ME WAS NOT MY FAULT

NAILS

Nails down my back
don't scare me
even when they leave trails
      in threes
      and fours
running down the length of my spine
making my roommate wonder
      what are they doing in that bathroom so long

I don't mind the soft touch of knuckles grazing cheeks
fingertips touching breast tips so gently
the orgasm is afraid to come

one out of every five times
I prefer that
slow
easy
kind of loving
that makes the body slide into itself
sleepy and complete
with the catlike purring of a puss
well stroked

but on the ordinary day
when I've written a good poem
or a fucked up poem
a poem I'm too ashamed to let the other poets see
I want a leash
      with my name on it
      attached to a collar with tiny silver studs
      to press into me
      when I attempt to escape

I want to wear cheap lingerie
so you can rip the lace into strips

you'll use to tie my hands together
and spank me
for exposing the details
of our not-so-ordinary sex life

and I think it's good to be 110 lbs
that way
you can get into my hard-to-reach-places easily
and I seriously doubt you can do that twister thing
with a woman much bigger than this—that thing
where I'm—I'm standing on the edge of the bath
and I'm—I'm not allowed
to hold the curtain rod—
and you
behind me
making me—

or that other thing
where I'm in the kitchen,
and you hoist me up on the counter by my knees
and dinner is a little bit later than we planned—

those days, I don't want quiet
I wouldn't know what to do with it
I like it when there are screams
        and battle-scars
        and trophies

that way before the war begins
I already know
what I'm about to fight for

LOVE

I've bought the bloody myth

swallowed that sucker
hairy legs and all
crawled careless into bed with a fantasy
and now I'm hopping antsy with expectation

      having drawn these crooked lines
in what looked to me like sand
my uncertain frame stands
hooked
on what I have been promised by the TV
by that saccharine ache Anita Baker
moans from a mass-produced CD

the game of happily ever after in love
is a cruel farce
      the lonely wish of a gullible asshole
somebody done told
a whole lot of silly lies to
love is nothing
but the by-product of a teenager
wagering hormonal changes
against the smell of his own diluted sperm
spilling innocent into his awkward palm

love is the alms
given to the poor to divert
focus from the difference
between the shacks that teachers live in
in Brooklyn
and the mansions that senators fuck young interns in
in Washington DC

I am just about ready to give up
on man
woman
dog and tree
the whole romantic tic is hogwash

the idiots
who look like they might still be in love
have only been together
for three weeks
and those lucky enough to have lasted more than a year
are rapidly shifting gears
towards chopping the shared
now dysfunctional cat
in two equal parts
so they can cart the rest of their shit
to the new apartment
they cannot afford by themselves

I am tired of searching for Ms. Right
                always something wrong
        with the one girl who likes me
too smart
too skinny
too much of a ninny
too short/too tall
too-much-of-a-mall-girl for my liking
too free/too taken/too I'm sorry I was mistaken
in my initial assessment of your sexuality
        sometimes
        I think I hang my hat too high
        for my own arms to reach them
which brings me back
to my original hypothesis
of love being somewhat like the perfect orgasm ·
        the trip there
is infinitely better than the letdown
of having already experienced it

             after the first
actualization of intercourse
there's no up to go from there
what is one to do with the sticky wet
of saliva
and vaginal fluid
and sweat
not drying fast enough
in the center of a lumpy futon
you are desperately trying to fall asleep on?

love
as I have understood it
is primarily disappointment
and hard work and very little return
so now I'm canvassing for volunteers
to go tar the cupid who conjured
the stupid concept
feather the fucker and leave the body to burn

MY JAMAICA

My love affair with Jamaica
has always been double-edged

two ends of a pimento candle
burning towards a slender middle
the indulgent heat pushing me off-center
        on this island
there has never been safe ground
the flat-cut of Liguanea
contrasts with the fluid shape of indigo mountains
Gordon Town frames the blue-black faces cleaning
dirty windscreens on Hope Road
        the hunger in their eyes eerie at twilight
        the dead breathing wistful flames at night

rolling across childhood memories
the raspy sound of my brother's breathing
reminds me that I must never rest
the uneven iron bed wasn't big enough
to hold my dreams—my fears
sweating through the polyester nightgown

water will always find its own level
my grandmother whispers
        sleep now—before the new day come find you
still looking into yesterday

Jamaica has always been harsh
hard words of rigid correction
connecting with the side of my head
        two fingers of water above the rice
        turn down the fire when the pot start boiling
        and gal-pickney must learn fi wash them under-clothes

the white uniforms hid the welts on my legs
the blue ties tempered the catholic purity
soft sister-hands encouraged the metal rosary
B+ was never acceptable in math
you want to sell cigarettes on the roadside?
finish you homework
and come get a piece of cornmeal puddin'

the land has always been lush
coconuts' husks split open to the rush of a moody sea

Sunday afternoons on the endless sand
pre-adolescent belly bottoms slit to reveal the red fruit
pulpy sweet but angry in captivity

Jamaica
has always loved me from a place of random beauty
women with wide cassava hips
and full, star-apple lips
women with strong hands
reaching beyond their own fears
to give their children courage
teaching them to stand straight-backed
in the absence of fathers who visit
with the smell of white rum in their words

my father has never loved women
with soft hands—my mother will show you the scars
still wrapped around her solid middle
banning her belly tight against visibility

this child will never be silent
I speak now
because my grandmother gave me my tongue
I speak now
because Jamaica has always given me
crosses I will have to bear alone

the only compass my mothers needle-sharp pain
shooting proud across my back
marked like a crab
Jamaica has always been able to find me
a thorn among the bloody hibiscus blooms
my Jamaica
has always been
the hardest poem to write

TWEET THIS, MOTHERFUCKER

In response to the man who tweeted, "You're a dirty carpet munching cunt that belongs in my kitchen, washing my dishes and cock. Your test-tube baby is a freak of nature. Write a poem about that. . ."

Obviously
you are a rotting dick/an asswipe
an open sore existing
among the worst tumors that plague humanity

you are an apology someone should have made
to women centuries ago

today you remain
a very good reason abortions should remain legal
and available
to every woman who finds herself
carrying the figurative fetus of your fetid misogyny

get the fuck out of my womb
you hater of your own origin
you forget you came from some woman's cunt
the pussy you so deride
provided a path for you
to get here spewing such sick soliloquy

your existence
also makes a good argument for capital punishment
only I hold myself
accountable to a more compassionate code of ethics
so I will refrain from advocating
for the archaic quartering of you
I will also resist the urge
to imagine you shackled in sequestered servitude
kneeling at the altar of some woman's holy punani
washing her feet with your mouth

only
I would not wish her the degradation
of your tongue on her flesh
your feet on her floors

I will spend my entire life
trying to protect my daughter
from the slime of your ignorance
the sweat of your hate
coward that you are
hiding behind the intangible shroud of the virtual
your keystrokes
are the only ones with any fucking power
impotent
unimportant little man
you splatter the male identity
with the putridity you exude
rotting apple/gonorrheal wound
refusing to heal/you would have us conclude
that most men are like you
but for the stellar examples in my life
I would think you the norm
your actions might inform the love I cradle
for those small boys in my circle
earnestly learning how to be better
than the monster you have chosen to be

far and away/Frankenstein
you frighten me
with your ability to keep breathing
your inclination to replicate
to recruit
to keep pressing the boot of your discrimination
upon the necks of generation after generation
after generation

the only thing that prevents me from raising arms
and going guerrilla after you with guns
is our collective dedication
to the eradication of your kind
across all the borders of feminism
and race/spaces hold wire against the throat of inequality
women resist you/heart and body
with cunts and collarbones
kill your cowardice
kitchens and bedrooms
we rebuke all you offer as fact

the act of tweeting something does not make it true
you ignorant motherfucker

you are only a narrow opinion
constructed poorly
in 140 characters/your cavalry
is not nearly as committed as mine

from Nairobi to New York City
from Kingston, Jamaica, to Jakarta
these litanies we are forced to compose
will stand as evidence
to your crumbling motherfucking tyranny
time will hold your actions
as crimes against humanity
as it was with every disease before you
the strongest/most admirable parts of being human
will keep adapting/over and over
watch us adapt/motherfucker
watch us morph/hatch/give birth to a power
reminiscent of Harriet Tubman and Sojourner Truth

history has already shown us
what doesn't kill us
will make our resistance stronger

can you hear me/motherfucker?
what doesn't kill us/will make our resistance stronger
what doesn't kill us/will make our resistance stronger
what doesn't kill us/will make our resistance stronger

IN RESPONSE TO DANISH

(the six-year-old Pakistani passenger who asked me why I write)

For myself—I tell her
for fear there might be nothing left
beyond this ritual
this excess of religion
the reason mankind loves condemnation
and images of a white male God

for Jamaica
the island that rejected me
for my fingers writing impossible sonnets
on the inner muscle of a female thigh

for the women I left there
bleeding for the zygote of that lust
aborted for just being

they still live there
far from the hands that pushed me
down the staircase with the broken banister
because we all need to push back at something
sometimes

for the skeletons I write
only in inked outlines
for the vibrator that crosses state lines with me
for the nights I sleep alone

for the man I left
because he could not understand
why I complained of cramping heavily one month

for my father
who has only ever wrapped his lips around my name

once
for my grandmother who hums it every morning
in prayer
for the fear of my mother
who might very well be mad
for the way I move my hands like her
when I speak
for the words that threaten insanity
if I do not speak out loud

for the child I hope to nurture from my navel
one day
for the world I will be afraid
to pass on to her
for my version of America
for the drunks who rest their conscience in open gutters before dawn
for denouncing Hitler
for South America
for History and Ayatolah
for the women who never loved me
for the ones who always loved me back
for Angela
and Anna-Lisa
for Asha and Andrea and Alexandra
for Arianna who writes happy poems
because she believes in dancing
for this alphabet of needs we swallow without fluid everyday
for Alejandra who lives in Austria
for Brent who went back to Trinidad
for the letter C
I cannot say her name
for fear of her safety
for Deean
for Elisha
for Fernando and Peter
and to move this poem along I write for Quraysh
and his sons

for Racquel who loved me when I chose not to love her back
for lost strangers
speaking in musical foreign tongues
for the violence we ignore
as long as it is not being done to us
for undoing those secrets our mothers' mothers
told us never to speak of
Malcolm who wrote his name the only way he could not spell slave
for Lorraine Hansberry
who always wrote like she was Black
for the young and the gifted
for the lack of causes that reflect us
for the surrender we refuse to write
for the dream
for the dried grapes of wrath
for the reasons so many shadows continue to exist
because the world will not accept
the people who live in fear behind them

LETTER TO MY FATHER

Father
the A-train is late again

      only moments to spare
and I find myself thinking of you
      penciled tall in my memory
        looming a full five feet from the ground
the rain pelting into me
slicking strands of hair to my aching neck
urging me to hold you responsible for the aborted weddings
the whispered stories about my mother
the gaping secret she tried to take with her to Canada

      I feel it now
digging into my memories
infant bruises bleeding muddles my mind if I pause
for more than a Manhattan minute
inking my pen with nostalgia
mocking my accent in America
the immigrant chewing the chalky flesh of an imported mango

on days like this you invade this need I have for women
      to swallow air with them
breathing backs curved taut against frightened bellies
silver spoons slipped easy into each other
reflecting the fury of the faces that are never quite sure
why they fit together so well
why the rightness of that geometry is so hard to defend

      on cold days like this
I yearn for the space between my grandmother's knees
the ancient smell of the amniotic soothing
as she pulled the tangles from my hair

with you
it was always winter
your white skin thin and yellow
showing me the ice inside

        on gray days like this
I want to make you see that I am
an excellent housekeeper
—hear me speak out
for little girls
—know
that I consort with rampant homosexuals
to taste the sorrow of women
who have not yet found their voices

beneath this thin sheet of ice—
        I want to beg you
look close at the girl who moves with the grace of a duck
ankles turned in just like you—
        shoulders never quite straight
look now, father—
        for soon, she will be gone

this girl loved by men
who gave of themselves
in bracelets and blood and being
walked in unholy places because they believed in me

they never quite measured up to what I imagined you to be

men always too sensitive
or too brash
wanted too much or too little
always fell short of your
rejection/money/spent/regular
exact figures unsure—
        I collected the stenciled square

on the first of every month
carried it carefully
a delicate confetti flake
          caressed it
fleshy thumb against flat paper
until your signature was almost invisible
          —the bank cashed it anyway

everybody knew
          father
I know you will never be proud

and I might someday stop
trying to make you out of this lettered train
rushing across the torn and twisted tracks
of this runaway daughter's recollection

till then
there is much to be done
this city is moving fast
and me?

I'm doing the best I can to keep up

JAMAICANS IN NEW YORK

Young, brash, and flag-waving for Labor Day
from Brooklyn, Queens, the Bronx
everybody on Eastern Parkway
hips rolling to the riot of the carnival sway
heads wrap tight in black
yellow paint on the body
a little bit o' green
just enough green inside them bag

New York is where Jamericans are happening

      Yes mi dear—
it has finally become hip to be the coconut
cool to know the lyrics of the latest reggae hit song

it won't be long now before Mr. Co-lin Powell
becomes "Colin" again
before we who pay all these taxes here convince
the IMF to forgive our country a debt we could never pay off
unless we start selling the darker skinned citizens again

Jamaica is the kind of place that foreigners fall in love with
during spring break, honeymoon, retirement, vacation
we are the perfect spot for tanning
for keeping tabs on Fidel Castro
for eating too much and sleeping too little
it is a place of servants and summer nights and all-inclusive hotels
      and still
         the natives leave The Rock in droves
         every year
we tear ourselves away
from the warm holiday white people spend years saving for
to become this metropolitan backdrop of props
hopping metal trains from Neanderthal to nigga
to international Nubian pop princess

but that warm holiday ain't never been for the poor
"sex on the beach" and the time to enjoy it
has always been reserved for backra and backra's wealthy friends
so some of us move further north
where we can afford to buy ill-fitting, overpriced clothes
where we can make money for records that refer to women as hos
we become hip when our accents are dipped
in US dollars
our collars become less blue
when we are less true to where we come from
this is how we have become whores of American appropriation

it was only forty years ago that West Indians
had to paint the preferred sound of America over their tongues

Black sunshine-boys of the nineteen sixties
had to bleed to become American
blow by ignorant blow they learned to fight back or run
from the teachers they could not tell about the white mouths that
      spat on them
about the frightened Black faces that could not claim them then

New Day that this is
Bob Marley has become
one of the most revered prophets of mainstream America
and every other bitch with dreads on her head is calling herself a
      Rasta

we are no longer other
            having been assimilated
bought and sold in this global economy of identities
the White House is steady working on
providing new targets for the Klu Klux Klan
genetically engineered hamburgers
are being marketed to the average Afghan
right now
the capture of Kabul is so much more exotic than Kingston

my bags now go unchecked in American airports
            only dark men
with names that sound like Osama, and Saddam, and Ali
stand at baggage checkpoints
soft shoes folded in hand
faces begging forgiveness for praying five times a day
for looking the way they look like the East
like the oil we need for these air-conditioned cars
these shuttles we keep trying to send to fucking Mars
these luxury planes
we need to carry bombs to tear down structures
that do not smell like the West

how many cultures can one country swallow
before it explodes like a very tall building or two
complete with a 747 rushing through
and when it finally crumbles
will all this have been worth the view?

KNOW WHEN TO FOLD

When I was six years old/my brother was everything to me

quintessential Jamaican boy/hard exterior/like we like our boys/
unforgiving
like Black men are encouraged to be
I adored him
frugal with his love as well as his money
his affections were conditional
I loved everything he did/and he loved him some Kenny Rogers
so I loved Kenny Rogers too

for nine years he was my only reflection
both of us brown/both abandoned by our mother
(him with lighter skin/his hair straighter than mine
we were similar enough to see ourselves in each other)
both hurt enough by the world to fiercely love each other
he loved me grudgingly
I adored him like an eager pup loves a reluctant owner

in charge of all we did
he made me sing country music
like we were born and raised in Memphis, Tennessee,
we spent whole afternoons
begging Ru-u-uby /not to take her love to town
singing Daytime Friends and Nighttime Lovers
like old drunks reliving tragic lives

he loved "The Gambler" most of all

you gotta know when to hold 'em/know when to fold 'em
know when to walk away/know when to run

he sang "The Gambler" like he was Kenny Rogers himself
I couldn't understand why he loved that song
but I would have followed him anywhere
so to please my brother/I sang "The Gambler" with gusto

then our mother returned and separated us

sent him to Mount Salem
left me in a place called Paradise and disappeared again
the distance between my brother and me/only two miles
might as well have been two thousand
we became single children of Sisyphus
pushing the rock of abandonment up disparate mountains

no more Kenny Rogers
he switched to reggae/I listened to Melissa Etheridge
        Sarah McLachlan/Meshell N'Degeocello
we both tried/so hard to remain close
but our love was never meant to survive
never meant for holiday dinners or lasting relationships
our life was marked for infrequent/awkward reunions laced with
sorrow/we lived everyday/pushing
against our deep desire for love
needing people/but guarding against it
such is the delicate wiring of emotional dysfunction

the few good times we had were complicated/rare/magical
        circa 1999
        we found compromise in Mariah Carey
        speeding/100 miles on the autobahn
        windows down we sang into the cold night
        felt so alone/suffered through alienation
        carried the weight on my own/had to be strong/so I believed

happy as I was/I remember thinking
—being a lesbian will one day cost me/my first love/my brother
the only boy whose opinion of me ever mattered

I needed my brother to love me/but I needed him to know me
      I took a chance/bated fate and told him
      all about the girlish collisions on campus
      the tacit lovers who went with me to illegal house parties/
in Jamaica
the pretty girls residing in the smallest closets on campus

      I couldn't be silent anymore/about any one of them
      I told my brother everything
      about the boys who assaulted me/about their hands
      their fingers
      their fists/he listened
      as I talked statistics
the rate at which they were killing people like me in Jamaica
frightened and resigned to losing him
      I told him I was about to be
out like a motherfucker
and my almost twin/both of us discarded by our mother
both half/breeds/both seeds of my mother's ill-conceived youth
only two years apart/my brother
who had no reason to/told me he loved me
my Jamaican boy/raised on a stout diet of violent homophobia/
said/I was his sister/so it didn't matter/and I didn't quite know
how to show him how lucky I felt to be his sister

I wanted to sing "The Gambler" right there and then/but the
moment wasn't right/so I silently swore to love him even more

I believed then/that our bond would survive everything
we loved each other/hard as we could
ill-matched/as siblings/witnesses to each other's pain/we
developed a routine of sustainability

whenever we disagreed about anything/he would mostly walk
away/and I would mostly not let him

at each fracture/I would remind him that all we had was each other/that we had survived our mother/that we could survive this

> so the last time we argued
> I was surprised how swiftly the way the tables turned
> without warning/you never see these things coming
> in an instant/we were again children
> forced to make beauty out of tragedy

the house of cards we constructed
collapsed/hurt and unable to find a way forward we both folded
bound and broken by all we had endured
we found ourselves unable to hold each other
angry and intractable my big brother walked away
and this time I let him
it's painfully poetic that
the contention was about our children
this irony proves everything about parenting and progeny
generational trauma cannot be side-stepped
today there is almost nothing but sadness between us
I know nothing of his present life
I imagine he knows nothing of mine
except what he would find inside these public/private/posts
if he cared to look/our childhood is now no more than a silent
scream
except for the odd memory triggered by an old playlist
cartwheeling me back to us/as children
unwittingly belting out our future
you gotta know when to hold 'em/know when to fold 'em
know when to walk away/know when to run...

SONG OF SURVIVAL

Strange wonder I survived
those blades serrated and beating
hard against the softest parts of me

so after all the first kisses
the last chances
the metered requiems
and the regret
      I left you
the white light of your smile
teeth glinting pearls and promises
palms holding razor sharp caresses—
slow kisses seeping into my breath

      I could not see
your hands filled with layers of my flesh
meshed with my desire
to see things work out
I stayed for much too long
ignored the blood leaving my body as salt/water
tears in tribute to what you took

I will never be able to give
that to anyone else again

      but sorrow is merely the beaten
back of our flawed ecstasies
flipped over and over
and over again
we stop knowing the difference
begin to give deference to one or the other
it does not matter
a woman can break the red organ pumping life
through the human body as easily as any man can

but for survival I have learned
nothing
except this song

the hot knife of betrayal slicing thick
through the mirrored expectations of me
disappointed in myself
and the *I am so sorry*'s—
the *I never really meant to hurt you*'s

yes, you did, you inconsiderate fuck!

I traveled three thousand miles and back for you
and you still fucked me over
        the back of your hand
        across my face
        my arms bruised under cotton
gauzy white and virgin
I denied my friends and their suggestions
carried your innocence on the small twist of my back

        the weight of you almost broke me

but the flat of your palms taught me
that I have always been stronger
than your fingers wrapped firm
around the chords in my frightened throat
and I have learnt that your cowardice
and your bullshit
and your continued attack on humanity
means that I must speak
wear the nectar-sweet scarring of your multiple orgasms on my
    sleeve
stripe them permanent so that others may see

for somewhere
        far away

and sometimes it is just in the room next door
a woman is swallowing the fist
of someone else's anger
and I am begging her to find the fury
to raise her hand in alarm
a weapon in defense of her dignity
pleading with her caged voice to rail in combat
against the midnight crack of her bones
the early morning split of your lips

the everyday spill of our daughter's blood
the death of more than one nation

if I have learned nothing else
from our bloody history together
I have learned to pitch
this voice far beyond
the secrets of our silent survival
to reach for the greater intention
to save more than my own life

LITANY OF DESIRE

Her body
is a litany of desires

I wrap them frail around
my body
ribs
striped and stretched
                    toward healing
            grotesque
            beautiful
            these sores
I carry them
fingers sticky and heavy with exactitude
flay the muscled sacrament
with wine
and water
and bread
and worship

I want you
litany
like bleeding
like a fire fanned open
like my legs
insistent
like fate
like salt
like memory

            tell them to me
                    your stories
tender to the touch
this
is what I have always wanted

                    from you
the cracked edge
of what has only
just begun to harden

I want you against time
and revelation
and beds too far away
            I want you
wanting me clothed in the absolution
of fangs and forks and fucks we shouldn't have
I want you buried in the belly of a blind belief
like Jonah
like an apostle
like Mary
like Joseph
            like God
I want your spirit
            made flesh
                        within me
            frail
and futile
I want to follow you
broken ground you
sound you hoarse from the flick
of my foreign tongue
like mud
and martyr
and mornings without sun

I want to quiet you
like quick
like cunt
like hollow
            like whole
I want to hold you
holy like prayer

like benediction
like intercession
like hallelujah
like hallelujah
like hallelujah
like   amen

SUPPLICATION

kiss me. like a girl.
make all of me wet and warm
—like a summer storm

ON JUMPING OFF LEDGES

You be up
in my gut like intestines
twisting away at my insides
like a blade
you be difficult to fade
like a discordant song composed to go higher
when it's ending
I play you incessant
over and over
to remind me
that we never began anything
really
never began
nothing

odd how I remember make-believe notes about you
       minor keys in succession
       of she wants me
       she wants me not
       it sure is crazy how I already fancy myself in love
       with the sound of you coming from Omaha
       or Idaho
       Michigan is the one place you made time for me
a bathroom in Frisco
is all I have
because I don't want to demand too much of you
don't want the slender bridge that connects us
to break because I had to show my lack
of home training
or patience
or the vision
to see that you were struggling with the decision
to see me before I dash off to Europe
or maybe because your woman wouldn't let you

go
all the way across the world
to see some strange woman read sonnets in Scotland

Denmark would be
the love song you might write
about us
        two Black girls on a ferry from
        Copenhagen to Malmö
we could circumvent fate
with the canal surrounding the city with almost no poverty
        wouldn't we be living pretty off the fat
of someone else's land

I want to know
what the small of my back
would feel like with your hand holding it
in Ireland

I want you to want me like you want
her to change
I want the freedom to write you like you want her to paint
        beautiful
and without hesitation
        I am lobbying
        for whole weekends in Washington
        to fuck you
        relentless in Berlin
and it not be a sin in Atlanta

the more practical parts of me recommend
resignation from this post of almost
lover
only sort of emotional
nearly-but-not-quite-fucking-you-friend

this cannot end well

so I have quietly decided to construct this
maybe-ultimatum-perhaps-even-final-farewell
before I find myself
three flights up on a broken fire escape
threatening to jump
or push you
over some ill-conceived ledge of impossibility.

TRAVELING

Amtrak don't have one palm tree—
the whole landscape of New England
pass invisible to the girl thinking she free
from the white flesh dancing the tanned
limbo on a seven-mile beach—
there was always something odd in the red skin
blistering with alms outreached
handing off useless American sins—
them times was real funny times—
the boys in a burlesque race for dimes
glinting in from tourists littering the sea
like they owned it more than we.

night travel more dread than memory
every passing light is a milestone
severing the bloodline from you own history,
every horn, the irreversible groan
of one more Pentecostal auntie fighting
not to disown me because my man
is a woman, every sound lighting
a fire for the bastard, the charlatan, the lesbian
who abandon paradise to write
poems about leaving paradise

nobody know how I fear this
slow-moving macabre dealing out death
with a Halloween grin and glow—
in certain cars you can hear me breathe
hissing like a machine shutting down
mocking me from small country to big town

the quiet confusion of the train
illustrates how distant my legs stand

from the warm marble drops of rain
rolling off from my changed hand

all this time and I still can't be sure
that leaving was the better thing
nearly ten years and still no cure
for the sad September fall of me wing

the blue sea beckoning and me, calling
back, soon come! All the while knowing,
I lying.

PASSING

Downtown Brooklyn is easy for me
long sheer skirts do little to hide my open legged stride
see-through button-down sleeveless blouses hug my bodice
so tight my nipples are barely concealed
by the carefully chosen push-up bra from Macy's

see, I'm a femme
a real lipstick lesbian
so I can pass—
smelling like a straight girl in my Victoria's Secret
satin panties pressing against the men who walk alongside me
passing—the way my yellow-skinned grandmother passed
as white women sat in judgment

on plantation stools overlooking fields
of cotton and sugarcane sweetened by gallons
of Black blood and sweat running down thick
between the full breasts of the women
who lay still as blue-eyed men pierced their hearts deep
through the folds joining their legs

it's Jay Street-Borough Hall
and my friend is in trouble
someone takes the time to notice
that the young boy is really a young girl
and the red, white, and blue jacket is not enough
to cover the tattoo on her belly
two naked women wrapped around each other
like pretzels that came out different from the rest

it takes two minutes for them to break two ribs
        one for her lover who passes all the time
        the other she keeps for herself

and as those bones set
her sorrow breaks wide open
because she knows SHE can never pass
she knows that butch bodies are too strong
too strange, too dark
like those bronze bodies that smell
too thickly of rebellions and revolutions
                    and we know that revolutions take time
and sacrifice and lives to turn this world around

sometimes it makes me angry
that they think I look like them
so they can convince themselves I am okay
but I hasten to show them the tangled wool between my thighs

and I am quick to remind them
that the funk from me only rises
when my woman touches me
that I can only come
when she calls my name

we need to let them know
we do not wish to pass as semi-white
or almost straight
or nearly normal
so we can hold down corporate jobs
stroking narrow-minded dicks
so we can be invited to family dinners
to disown our brothers and sisters who cannot pass
who will not pass

we must let them know
that after the broken bones have healed
that we will still be here
that long after the bruised hearts have ceased to hurt
we will still be here and long,

long after our mothers no longer weep
we will still be here
still gay
still Black
still survivors in the face of this blatant bigotry
that will one day force us to lace arms and strike back

SEPTEMBER IN NEW YORK

The collapsing towers
punctuated the 2001 summer like a period
foreboding

the black smoke curling perpetual thriller
    on the screen would mean
terror for so many
    reporters
watching horrified/weeping/dumbfounded
as body after body flew through the glass windows
    amidst the cement dust faces
    strangers held fast to each other
    the unspoken boundaries between New Yorkers
    disappeared/New Yorkers hugged
    coughed up the heavy air
    meandered among the soot-covered cars
    the words Hijab/Jihad/Taliban were not yet known
    there was only the checkpoint traffic jams
    the unsolicited notes we wrote
    to long forgotten colleagues/cousins
coworkers gave each other
the benefit of the doubt
    enemies shouted pleasant greetings
    across the eerily quiet platform
    worn and disheveled/with nothing else to lose
    we were determined to love our neighbors

even the skeptics began to believe it might last

    —but politicians/and opportunistic charlatans
    turned the tide quick to terror
a country made sick with talk of fear
of further attacks
folded as our leaders stacked the reasons we had to

smoke them out
root the evildoers out of their caves
within weeks boys barely shaving were bundled off
to wars in places unpronounceable
angry weapons with friendly names
were quickly aimed
at ordinary people/in Queens/in Brixton/in Kandahar

in New York
the smattering of protests were skillfully deflected
        —American lives were at stake
        something has to be done
        America needed to act
        that was a fact
images of villages dodging
cluster bombs
smart bombs
projectile bombs dominated the news
        the narrative of cowboys killing savages
        droned on while the streets of Manhattan
displayed crudely constructed posters
        making martyrs of the missing
        —September will always
remember the shell-shocked mourners
the towers/buckling/falling
the long hours spent calling hotlines
the months of not knowing
who had been at work that week
who had been fired the week before

the conspiracy theories threatened the worst in us
the religious rallied for blood
the exodus from Manhattan spiked the cost of apartments
        in Brooklyn
        in Astoria
        in Jersey City
almost a decade later

the poor can no longer afford their own homes
every port/every bridge/every tunnel
      every airport on the planet
regulates computers/liquids/gels/creams
shoes/belts/jackets/coats/hats/bags
everything is examined for irregularities
everyone must be transparent
one-quart resealable polyethylene plastic bags

every year September holds still
the moment
before 9/11/after 9/11
we gather/at the end of summer
pray
reflect/remember the day
the New York skyline fractured
and sent the rest of the world
spinning
to piece itself together again

TAKE BACK THE NIGHT

TSUNAMI RISING

#MeToo

In the balance of human biology
all bodies are created equal
everybody is about seventy percent water
regardless of race/religion
gender/sex or sexual orientation
we all die after seven days/without drink

but the idiots obsessed with category have decided
that a double X chromosome designates me
subordinate to those with an X and a Y
intersect those two X's/with the fact of my Blackness
and my existence is coded as dangerous/hostile
a direct threat/to the endurance of the white patriarchy
and everybody knows white men have spent centuries
appropriating what they wanted
the gold they found in Africa/was not enough
so they packed human bodies/head to toe
submerged in a swamp of our own urine and feces
they dragged us across violent waters
many of us drowned
our young/rather than let them live
at the mercy of white men/and their sons
and their grandsons, and their grandson's sons

to keep breathing
some of us became one-dimensional
in the public imagination/in real life/in books
we had to become one thing or the other
spinster/or mother
virgin/or victim/damsel/or whore

some of us went underground/for centuries
some of us let go/slipping away into the sunken place

others revolted/took up arms
crawled through sewage/defied geography
to build new lives in new cities

in Brooklyn/I spend my nights reading tales of Nubians
bathing naked in the Nile/Kushite queens
equal to kings/all of them praying to a Black woman named Isis
the most powerful/goddess among gods
I imagine/if I were her/I would use my might
to smite every motherfucker
whoever looked at a little girl with lust in his flesh
I would exact vengeance on behalf of every
Black woman who has disproportionately borne
the weight of racial and sexual violence
while everyone in the suffragette movement
and the Black civil rights movement
and the LGBT movement
turned a blind eye
to her swollen lips mouthing/me too
someone please help me
get him off me/me too/me too/me too

for centuries we have endured
the culture of rape and racism combined
for centuries the world has stood silent
while Black women and girls were bullied
by Black men and white men/white women alike
for centuries/anyone who wanted to hit something
or own someone/they could decide we were it
without consequence/anyone could tag
the Black woman/the dark girl/the universal punching bag

for centuries/rape was a word Black mothers
never spoke aloud
but every daughter knew what it meant
lie still/it will pass/keep quiet
ignore the girl who screams too loudly

don't you dare shame this good Black family
then something brilliant happened
a Black woman named Tarana Burke
inspired wealthy white women
to say #MeToo

herein wriggles the strange rubric
of America's particular strain of racism
ironically/the viral mobility of the #MeToo hashtag
was only possible because a white woman with power
retweeted a Black woman's words
two words which unleashed a wildfire of public testimony
pulling the shroud of sexual violation from the shadows
shoving it onto prime time TV
yet/twelve years after Tarana Burke's #MeToo moment
Black women are still largely missing
from the public dialogue about sexual assault

we are so tired of being disregarded
if you gave Black feminists room to speak honestly
this is the letter we might pen to the white feminists
whose crying consistently drowns out the sound of our suffering

dear weeping white women
even as we cannot find safe space to show you
where or when or how we were torn open
we are only holding our sorrow
to keep our hearts from imploding
we are unable to process our pain with you
because we are exhausted from centuries
of holding you and your children
we have a hard time trusting you
because you all have never been able to stand by us
we are so tired of explaining ourselves
if you wish to know more about the genesis of our rage
please Google us/or read bell hooks
or Brittany Cooper

or the blogs of the bevy of Black women writers
your white publishers are too afraid to publish

for centuries
we have been carrying the weight of your white fragility
year after year marching for everyone else's freedom
protesting for everybody's privilege/but ours
well/this crazy/mad/gaggle of global witches/and hags
are done braiding beads of silent acceptance
simply put/in this century
we intend to take up more motherfucking space
sincerely/Black womanists

Black women are crafting a collective response
to centuries of being under everybody's water
We are a rising tsunami of fury come back
to take back what was carried away/without consent

and while we're here being candid
I might as well confess to you
that I don't give a fuck if you don't like me/my big mouth
Black like my lover's ass
has not endeared me to the gatekeepers of white civility
my proclivity to speak the unspeakable is essentially the only
defense I have against
the indefensible violence of your man—made history

in my house
there is no shadowtalk of birds or bees
we trade indecipherable metaphors
for concrete words that do not confuse my daughter
I tell her/your mouth/your elbow
your hair/your arms/your legs
your vagina/your whole body belongs to no one but you
and if ever you feel even a tiny bit unsafe
you open your mouth and scream for help
if anybody/anybody at all

does anything that makes you feel uncomfortable
you tell me/I will always believe you

in a world that regularly demonstrates how much it hates you
this is what it means to be assigned the label of Black and girl

and yet/we continue to survive
to thrive/arrive into adulthood with the ability to laugh
and love and wear hoop earrings
and tight skirts/to found social movements
to liberate other motherfuckers from bondage
if any of this sounds like I'm speaking your story
this poem be for you/my love
if ever you have had to argue/that you are no less deserving
than your white counterpart/I am talking to you

if you have ever been inspired by the magic of Black women
with thighs and asses that move mountains in their stride
if you have ever been told you speak too fiercely
from the thick lip of your own truth
if you've ever been called a girl/like it was an insult
if you've ever been called bitch
step forward
if you are itching to light a fucking bonfire
in the house of the white patriarchy
come stand with Black women/now
if you want to be free like Harriet Tubman
weapon in hand/wading through unfriendly waters
her power compelling the freedom
of even those who did not want to be free
if you desire to be confrontational like Sojourner
if you wish to be audacious like Audre
antagonistic like Angela
gangsta like Winnie Mandela
angry like Assata Shakur
come roar with us at our rallies
sit beside us/in school

sing with us in church/stand with us/where it matters
vote/with us and for us/at the polls
travel with us/in the virtual
in the flesh
over these waters they have used against us as weapons
across the lands of this rock we all call home
let us use fire to crack
the ground wide open with an uprising
that will never again
die down
no more water/*The Fire* Next *Time*/no more water/*The Fire* This
Time

NOT MY PRESIDENT

Every time I step to a microphone
I develop an uncontrollable itch to shout
Donald J. Drumpf is not my president

and that's not just because I didn't vote for the fool
not just because he's become the latest tool
members of the contemporary Klan
pull out of from their modern day sheets to remind us
of when their cloths covered this land with the brutal hand
of white racist terror

If you have ever had to dress down some
Melanin-challenged motherfucker
talking 'bout all lives matter—
raise your right hand and say amen

so you know exactly what I mean when I say
Donald J. Trump cannot be recognized as no motherfucking
president

first of all
he's been breathing on this planet for seventy years
and still has the vocabulary of a third grader
not to mention his mouth always looks to me
like an incontinent asshole that can't hold in its own bullshit
spewing the septic defecation of ignorance and discrimination
contaminating the already polluted air with inarticulate
entitlement
steady providing validation
for all the other them/other white men who feel like
equal opportunity for anyone else
means we are trying to motherfucking oppress them

Donald J. Trump could never be my president
because he began his political career
by questioning the legitimacy of the first Black president
elected in a country
built upon the hard-working backs of Africans Americans
he could never be my president
because he had the gall to call for Barack Obama's birth papers
as if this were 1831 and he was one of them cruel white men
free to grab any Black body and demand documents

in the America we are currently fighting to create
men like that can no more lead us
than can a predominantly white police force protect
the Black descendants of the very brown bodies they enslaved
to gain the racial advantage they refuse to let go of
no matter how obvious it is—that in America/race and opportunity
are linked/like poverty and the prison system
like rape and a woman's right to choose
like who has wealth and who pays the least taxes
like gerrymandering and who gets the right to vote

it's time for poor white folks to admit
they've all been sold a six for a nine

this con artistry of race and sex and economy isn't new
Donald J. Trump is just another white knot in the noose
they keep tying around the necks of the disadvantaged majority
just another fairy tale in the elaborate inheritance of lies
they sell to anyone who isn't rich
and white and longing for the good old days
when racially cloaked narratives of nationality
was the only history available to average Americans
fed to them/to keep them from being woke
to keep them from poking too deeply
into whose pockets most of the wealth that ordinary people work for
from 9 to 5 everyday in this country/goes
Black people have had enough of this systematic bullshit

between the five hundred years of unrelenting racism
and the recent rise of this fake-ass over-tanned idiotic orangutan
Black bodies have got no more tears left to cry
we ready to try some next level shit
to resurrect some Black Panther
Angela Davis
Assata Shakur shit

I'm willing to bet the same is true the rest of y'all motherfuckers
I'm willing to bet you know that
the state of things as they are/is unacceptable
having spent my whole life fighting for better than this
I refuse to give deference
to this walking, shameful evidence of what fear
and prejudice
and a lil Russian interference/can birth in a nation
obviously asleep at the wheel of our own democratic elections

Donald J. Trump is not my president
because his tenure in the Whitehouse is a result of unchecked sexism
a culture of rape
and the ever present undercurrents
of the newly emerging twenty-first century ku klux klan
Donald J. Trump is not my president
because he wants to disappear our Muslim neighbors
because he wants to deport Mexican American families
because he fails to recognize that the only Americans
who are not immigrant Americans are Native Americans
he is not my president because he sexualizes his own daughter
he will never be my president
because I want to clearly demonstrate to my daughter
that a man who boasts about grabbing women by their vaginas
without their permission/does not ever deserve her respect
no matter who he is/or how rich he says he is
that even though that egotistical airhead
masterminded and pulled off the greatest political coup
in the history of modern elections

he remains nothing/but an illegitimate, embarrassing burden
I hope we won't have to have to carry for four whole years

every time I see this orange snake slithering around on my screen
I want to break my fucking TV
rip it off the wall and let it fall from my fifth floor apartment
I wish I could just close my eyes and pretend
that none of this is happening

but if we do not keep our eyes open
the consequences will be catastrophic
every kind of resistance is necessary
when the arm of injustice persists
we have to develop new ways to resist
we have to keep trying/keep changing tactics

we have to find a way to impeach this motherfucker

we cannot be discouraged by these political tricks of distraction
it will take longer than we anticipated
to get this fucker off our TVs/out of office
and outside our collective consciousness
it could take a year/or two or—God help us—it could take four
but no matter how long it takes
we have to keep to the truth of what we know
—this buffoon cannot lead
so we cannot follow him to the sordid places he would have us go

no matter how normalized the actions
of this incredibly imbecilic and inhumane administration has
    become
no matter how numb we become to what the news anchors say
you have to say something different to yourself
Donald J. Trump is not my president
has never been my president
will never be my president
make it a mantra

say it to your fish
your parrot
your republican counterparts/say it over and over again/to them
and one day/when everyone else sees
he's no more than a snake oil salesman
no more than Cheeto-dusted Freddie Krueger
invading every aspect of our lives
like all the great walls of divisiveness built before him
he will fall/revealing the yellow bellies of all those
who brought him to power
and whoever is responsible
be it Vladimir/of one of them funny looking Trump children
whoever it is/that Iago motherfucker
will have to answer to the rest of humanity
for this small-handed wrinkle
in this bumboclaat warp in time

OPEN LETTER TO THE MEDIA

*Especially the news networks that covered the United States' 2003
invasion of Iraq*

Dear anchors and editors etc.
          if you were to summon me
for fifteen minutes of on-air conversation
on any topic of your choosing
I would arrive on time
in my most revolutionary gear
        because a few seconds of fame is a lot of power
        in these times of digitally altered truths
we underground runners flirting seductive with the mainstream
have long since known the value of your coveted reviews

but I cannot
with any freedom or integrity of conscience
accept your portrayal of Iraqi stories
I am resisting your sporty reportage of veiled mothers
holding malnourished babies still warm
from the bloody bullet pushed patriotic
through their already ailing bodies

your headlines remove the dignity
from poor people's dreams
when you endorse the bombing of Baghdad
basura
and Um Qasr

we know nothing of these places
but what you choose to tell us
your arrogance scrolling across the bottom of my screen—
fictional accounts embedded in the jaunts of journalists joyriding
on the backs of tanks
the old lie painted on the faces of boys barely fucking yet
Dulce et Decorum est!

honor cannot dry the tears of a mother
a wife
a daughter with a folded flag standing in for her father
these are the horrors of a story still unfolding
of tiny fingers exploding still holding unseasoned rice cakes
the terrors of every war—and still you cannot tell me
what we are so desperately fighting for

information is a weapon and you
vox populi turned propaganda machine
have turned the nozzle against us
nothing is to be trusted
in your make-believe-real-TV-movies

I am tired of flipping from correspondent
to dishonest correspondent
your tall tales of metal statues falling are not new
American idols fall all the time on primetime TV
and in between we watch
young Black men eating the raw testicles
of buffalos while presidents give speeches
that inject pride into a more shameful history than you are willing
to admit

we pay way too much
for your opinions disguised as news
you are no different from our politicians jerking off
in the mouths of an underage population
we are tired of your backhanded rhetoric
your logo-printed views
we need a force who is unafraid to present the news
as it occurs
we need more than your carefully crafted letters
better we whisper the revolution from ear to ear
better we turn the volume down and have more sex
better to fuck
than to tuck our bare feet under the inertia

of these misled masses
better to stick our tongues up each other's asses
than sit on our couch with our mouths wide open
inhaling the funk your artificially expelled
caca-
phony of gasses

LETTER TO THE REMAINING
ABORIGINES IN AUSTRALIA

> *I am the terrorist I must disarm.*
>
> —June Jordan

My whole life
National Geographic has sold your tribal markings
as the fashion of Down Under

two days sunning under the Sydney sky I have seen
no trace of your decorated faces
only the backs of these shadows sleeping drunk
on the city's sidewalks
       not so much beggars as
people prevented from choosing
their own destiny

       not alone in the global community
the Seminoles
reflect your predicament in Florida
       Zulus prance their image on silver coins
for tourism in South Africa
       not one Arawak remains mirrored in my Jamaica

at night
you disappear into the dark of Hyde Park
left of Liverpool
north of Elizabeth Street
modern reality smeared with the stains of the Old Empire

       the educated in New Delhi still speak
      English with a British accent
      it is no accident that Blair and Bush
have buried the transatlantic hatchet

to pool resources
in response to the emerging head of a United States of Europe

all eyes are on the East
new age Napoleons poised toward possession
       —savage intentions
       make hidden weapons of the bodies
       of teenagers in Qatar

       the poor in Tehran watch helpless
       as CNN reports the bloody deaths of ordinary Israelis
       kneeling for prayer in Tel Aviv
the collective heart of the West
hardens against Palestinians clawing
body parts from the rubble of Arafat's last
argument with Sharon

nothing interrupts the boyish
bickering—the blatant bartering of lives
—soldiers/refugees
victims of indifferent hands
carving artificial borders across lands
that had no boundaries before those palms landed

responsibility washes all our hands
with the guilt of association
if there is to be peace with compassion
it must begin with the me

to quote the late June Jordan
I am the terrorist I must disarm

each well-fed body must stand trial
for crimes of poverty and violence against the other

each invisible face
must be found and accounted for

the untouchable
the leper
the woman
the orphan
the Cuban
the faggot
the face
pushed to the edge of existence

I am the Jamaican
hunting for signs of the Aboriginal in Australia
I know you are still connected to this land
show yourselves
as magic or moonlight
or master plan
      I imagine
        an ordinary band of bodies
rising up strange among these buildings like blades of grass
breaking open the tinted windows
rewriting your true history on the new
transparent glass

TAKE BACK THE NIGHT

For D'bi Young
and the blue girl who cannot acknowledge me
and Sloane
and Tia Honey Bee
and Gloworm
and all the voices
still screaming survival against the odds

It's dark again
and the familiar demons wrest my innards
low down
the slow moan of flesh being ripped

innocence/awkward and torn
we are all sworn to secrecy

don't tell
don't say nothin to nobody

nobody will believe it happened to you
blue/bruises

some of us bled
the rest carried the broken blood vessels in braille
rail silent against
a truth constructed

swallow the scum of him
in the dark
park the sniveling/tear-stained lump that you are
under the smiles

the tales of *I am* so *managing*

decades later
the flashes will blind your ability to love
tell you
you do not deserve the passion
the candor
the ardor of any love that holds you without violence

you will second-guess yourself
shelve the little girl calling for help

she lost her voice under that muffled theft
she cried out
and her throat broke

now she don't sing unless something is hurting
how we mask that thing

fling it grinning under the facade of flirting
girding our loins with lust/tainted with silences

grief
thief that he was/the prints of him remain

for years
I was afraid of the dark
still cannot sleep too deeply

sex and my body
must always be watched/closely

slowly walks the healing of all this bad feeling
fueling fears of not being good enough

pretty enough
smart enough
quick enough

to stop him from scarring that small body

how I still sweat that moment before
could I have stopped it

could I have saved me
had I screamed

shouted
mouthed a mantra like

let me go you fucking fuck
leave me here
unbroken
unbent
unspent from your hands around my innocence

let me go
let me go
let me go

if I had been able to voice it
make him listen
make him stop

would I now be whole/able to laugh without fangs
fuck without hang-ups

bang bang
before the gun of him went off

was there anything I could have said
read
seen
heard to make him let me go

before the shudders
and the things that go bump in the dark

before I became afraid of my own pleasure
my own measure of being strong
and woman

before my mother
and her absence
before my aunt

and how powerless she felt
before she knelt before God and made me the sinner

before I thought being thinner would make it better
before these unwritten letters marking my bruised skin

before I said no
the first time

before he ignored me
before they jumped me

before I froze
before he rose up and engulfed me

was I anything then
what am I now
        now that I have found this voice
        now that I know I had no choice
        now that I can say out loud

these scars are battles in a war I am winning
        now that I am able to say
these wars are nothing to the breadth of my survival
now that I am sure my arrival here
was no accident

now that I see that I am far from being spent
now that I know that this mouth

is only a beginning

a low moan
a groan breaking sound and barrier

skin and glass
I am finally able to see through me

I am only a place to let the light in
The dark ain't got nothing on this bitch

witch that I am
I can see you coming motherfuckers
I recognize you

and you will never be able to silence my daughter

she will know that whatever you do to her
is nothing to what we intend to do to you

in return she will climb these hills of impossible memories
she will see you/coming

you will not be unfamiliar
we will speak of you

we will belch you bile and bulbous from our mouths
we will talk as if you are only breath

the end of your reign is certain
we will break your violent cycle
we have already found our voice
be advised we are now marching
we are women roaring
consider yourself notified
of our intent to take back the night

WORDS LIKE RAPE

1.

Words like rape, he said
are best omitted
from a carefully crafted poem

without meter or much matter for serious scansion
the accusatory imagery
runs inflammatory—
prejudicial

in short
good verse cannot survive the violence
of a named horror

if you do not say it
the terror grows
exponentially—

rendering the occurrence
a contained operatic
beauty

2.

She wanted to write down
names
place body parts at particular angles
to better depict the terror

the scream she swallowed with his saliva
his soft tongue like raw fish
forcing open her unwilling mouth.

he must have broken skin with his insistence
his rough fingers sliding under surfaces
he had no right to feed on her like she wasn't flesh

she bled like a motherfucker when he entered

red and semen
making metaphors of her innocence

rape
was the one word that sufficed

rape
contained the shame of his weight
his pubic hairs bruising the delicate center of her clit
the trunk of him
driving back and forth—the unnamed horror splitting her open
like an unripened fruit

the crisp finality of that sound
rape
made him into a thing she might breathe through

the word rape
gave meaning to the grunting
the gargantuan heave of him spilling all he could into her

rape
was a word she could say out loud

when the disconnected details would not be vomited up
she could retch the word
rape

every time she uttered the word
rape—

      yes that man right there
      he raped me

      —she grew
      every time she said it, he
      raped me

      her terror abated
      exponentially

      rendering her survival
      an uncontained operatic beauty

MIDNIGHT–MORNING

Sleep softened
and seventeen thousand miles
removed
your voice shrinks these skyscrapers in Sydney
smaller than your moonlit apartment in Brooklyn,
New York walls
closed cold round your frame snuggled
deep between the pages of the bed we warmed together
not quite two weeks ago

the memory haunts—a yearning
blooming wild orchids and peach pie—

I get high from the soft parts of you unfolding
flesh and fiction presenting themselves
as poetry

even with these strange
kilometers cobbling the avenues
that separate our dreams
spider monkeys leap playful in performance
from reality to hope
and the future bleeds oceans of possibility
          —long tails
stroking slow caresses
set to Nina Simone in concert
          —ragged photographs of children dangling
from the edge of villages
built on odd objects
and tales of how we came to be
this quiet calligraphy of balance and beauty
          —sleep softened
          and seventeen thousand miles
          removed

you dissolve me/snowflakes swallowing sunlight
        the sound of us
        spanning the distance
sweat/sweet/pooling round these skyscrapers snuggled
between Melbourne and these moments
marked with safety and surrender
morning is still a meander of hours away
and I am already drunk
on the smell of you
waking

ON BECOMING THIRTY

I am inching into thirty
and my body thickens
a lyric of many measures
the chorus inside me swells
to meet my grandmother's stoic silence
        her hips have always been wider than mine
        wider than my mother's

Under the influence of a distant song
our footprints depress the earth in different time zones
the collective visible only in fragments—people and places
no one knows anymore

        I am affected by women who age beautifully
        women who sing off-key in public places, in bathrooms,
        in the absence of fathers and dead sons
        the women in my family ingest convention like duty

Sacrifice is the only way we know how to say *I love you* to our
daughters.

        In my small world
        Mama Lou begat Bernice
        who begat Hazel
        who begat me before she was forced to flee
        the barbed wire of poverty; long hours laboring
        for someone else's children
she sacrificed her own
for a chance beyond this ordered natured of things
tradition makes it impossible
to pave a pathway if you are a woman—if you chose
not to wear the dress rehearsal of wife
in some places *husband* is just another way to write
        warden

on the walls constructed around little girls.

my mother chose freedom!

and if I were not so busy being left behind
I would play the drums for the price of her liberty
tell you of her nights spent tossing in strange beds
hollow panels for headboards,
dark halls echoing the names she would spend three decades
trying to forget

the smell of Julie mangoes still remind her of her mother
she buckles under my anger, forgiveness extends to her only
through my German sister
who knows nothing of Jamaica
ninety miles off the coast of Castro's Cuba.

these women have always walked ahead of me
hope moving their children secure towards a dream
of this America
(poor people will do anything to get a US visa)

and still I grow older
four gray hairs shoot silver from my scalp
        I am beginning to look like my grandmother
        only I dance
        visibly out of step with time as we know it
        loop my arms around the faces that refuse to see me

        in tribute to Louise and Bernice who stayed
I raise my fist for me
for my mother who had the courage to leave

the lack of words between us reminds me
I come from a line of women with dark scars for last names
        women who sing in secret chorus across blue waters
        women who are quick to tell me

time has always been longer than rope

these women
teach me to play my own part of this endless song

SPEECH DELIVERED IN CHICAGO
AT 2006 GAY GAMES

Being queer has no bearing on race.
True love is never affected by color.

—*My white publicist*

I curb the flashes of me crashing across the table
to knock his blond skin
from Manhattan to Montego Bay
to bear witness to the bloody beatings
of brown boys
accused of the crime of buggery

amidst the newfangled fads and fallacies
the new age claims
that sexual and racial freedom has finally come for all—
these under-informed
self-congratulating
pseudo-intellectual utterances
reflect how apolitical the left has become

it is now commonplace to hear young activists say
the terms lesbian and Black and radical
come across as confrontational
why can't people just be people?

tongue and courage tied with fear
I am at once livid, ashamed, and paralyzed
by the neo-conservatism breeding malicious amongst us

Gay
Lesbian
Bisexual
Transgender
Ally
Questioning

Two-spirit
Gender non-conforming—every year we add a new letter
   yet every day
I become more and more afraid to say
Black or woman—every day
under the pretense of unity
I swallow something I should have said
about the epidemic of AIDS in Africa
or the violence against teenage girls in East New York
or the mortality rate of young boys on the south side of Chicago

even in friendly conversation
I have to rein in the bell hooks-ian urge·
to kill motherfuckers who say stupid shit to me
all day, bitter branches of things I cannot say out loud
sprout deviant from my neck

fuck-you-you-fucking-racist-sexist-turd
fuck you for crying about homophobia
while you exploit the desperation of undocumented immigrants
to clean your hallways
bathe your children and cook your dinner
for less than you and I spend on our tax-deductible lunch!

I want to scream out loud
all oppression is connected, you dick

at the heart of every political action in history
stood the dykes who were feminists
the antiracists who were gay rights activists
the men who believed being vulnerable
could only make our community stronger

as the violence against us increases
where are the LGBT centers in those neighborhoods
where assaults occur most frequently?
as the tide of the Supreme Court changes

where are the marches
to support a woman's right to an abortion?
and what are we doing about health insurance
for those who can least afford it?

HIV/AIDS was once a reason for gay white men to ACT UP
now your indifference spells the death
of straight Black women
and imprisoned Latino boys
apparently
if the tragedy does not immediately impact you
you don't give a fuck

a revolution once pregnant with expectation
flounders
apathetic and individualistic
no one knows where to vote
or what to vote for anymore

the faces that now represent us
have begun to look like the ones who used to burn crosses
and beat bulldaggers and fuck faggots up the ass
with loaded guns

the companies that sponsor our events
do not honor the way we live or love
or dance or pray
progressive politicians still dance around
the issue of gay parenting
and the term marriage is reserved
for those unions sanctioned by a church-controlled state

for all the landmarks we celebrate
we are still niggers
and faggots
and minstrel references for jokes
created on the funny pages of a white, heteronormative world

the current leftist manifesto
is a corporate agenda
and outside that agenda
a young boy dressed in drag is swallowing semen
so he can pay for dinner
a woman is beaten every twelve seconds
every two minutes
a girl is raped somewhere in America

and while we stand here well-dressed and rejoicing
in India
in China
in South America—a small child cuts the cloth
to construct that new shirt/that new shoe
that old imperialism held upright
by the misuse of impoverished lives

gather round ye fags, dykes, trannies
—and all those committed to radical social change
we are not simply at a political crossroad
we are buried knee-deep in the quagmire
of a battle for our very humanity

the powers that have always been have already come
for the Jew, the communist, and the trade unionist
the time to act is now!
Now! while there are still ways that we can fight
Now! because the rights that are left are so very few
Now! because it is the right thing to do
Now! before you open the door to find
they have finally come for you

CATALOGUE THE INSANITY

Catalogue your insanity
type the small words
push them from you
fingers and feet
and fury first
find the flippant denial
affirm it

bend
forget what you used to call her
learn the name of her new lover
write it on wax paper
burn it

forget the smell of her cunt
carry one poem to orgasm

erase the lines

catalogue the blood
drink the solution with intent
it was meant to be so
accept it
chant the inevitable and fold her picture in three

tear into the center of her face
copy the broken image
and send it to her
imagine her happy
smile slitting the frame

imagine her in Iowa
cornfields bending beneath another's hand
the soft land warming her back

catalogue her leaving
admit that she was never there
imagine her driving
haiku scattered from Denver
to Kentucky to Khartoum

construct a betrayal
make it a thing of unspeakable beauty
forgive her
slit your wrists
survive

count the number of times you have kissed her
multiply by three

imagine she kisses Iowa
five times more than that

pack
unpack
pull your shoestrings tighter than you need to
shave your head
move to Indianapolis
buy a dog
call her impossible
call her cell phone
hang up
call again

obsess
fuck other women who remind you of her
study their scent

shower less
stare at strangers
slip in and out of reality

do not explain yourself
survive

sleep with a man
swallow your fist
feel
survive

scrape the flesh from your unstable legs
abort the skeleton that stands there

ingest one gallon of paraffin
light a match from the box she left by your bedside

imagine her happy
then inhale

LESBIAN CHASING STRAIGHT

I told her
I liked the way she made that pink push up bra look intellectual—
and she laughed at me
beautiful
confident
deadly
she turned her color-treated blow-dried
bone-straight, just-curled arrogance the other way and roared

I almost told her—*If you didn't have that perm, you'd be perfect*
—only a scorned woman's opinion
it hangs on the uncertain balance of her laughter
still I wanted to go after her/beg her to sit with me awhile
lip-stick that smile to the tip of my pen
maybe then she would allow my forefingers
to construct the perfect poem on the hollows her elbows
the line of her neck made me want to paint her
brush-tattoo words up the inside of her ankle
tongue-caress metered shadows under her knees
how I wanted to please that woman
with the things I have learned to do to a body

But straight girls require more than the catchy lesbian line
they need more than the average stitch
in these times of weak-kneed freedoms
the bi-curious require a puss's whole nine lives
as they move in for the kill
it is a skill they perfect in the practice of rejection
it is the only protection they know in a world
where ladies are encouraged to toe the only line allowed

The slow grind of her heels sank into my wilting desire
as she spun away perfume and attitude swirling
the lines in my head twirling to the lift of her skirt

a boy I kissed once (perhaps twice)
told me that straight girls require work and study
and a different kind of program
in the moment I have refreshed myself
with the details of the curriculum for lesbian chasing straight:

rule # 1. You have to be platonic first
means you are nothing more than a friend
rule # 2. You cannot bend rule # 1 for the first three months
everything must be the same as you began until she adjusts
the plan is really to wait until there is a crack
in the lack of respect her boyfriend has for her
you must reinforce how she deserves so much better
you must have a vision
be ready to make quick decisions in the interest of her time
offer her your money
the comfort of your bed
save the bold statement of intent for when she is lying there
bent double with the need to be held
cradle her
tell her she is beautiful in the least objective language of your lust
stroke her
go gently toward her light spaces
kiss her hands—resist the urge to ask her to go down on all fours
drink beer from a brown bottle
or recite twentieth-century prose while she is being entered

do not insist on the norm of versatility right away
do not expect her to become that run-of-the-mill-dyke
with the 11½ multicolored plus one flesh colored dildo
the two essays on Middle American homophobia
three multi-speed vibrators
each with converters for Northern Europe
England and Australia—all rechargeable
avoid talk of the fluorescent butt plug right away
wait until you have had her
glowing in the stairwell with the lights turned on

her belly on your back
her back atop the ground
there will be time enough to show her how
lesbian sex has a way of being outrageous
what with the bedposts and those handcuffs
with the fur in the middle
wet spots and warm rags applied between giggles

straight girls are unable to swallow the entire syllabus in the first
class

so I resisted the urge to go after her
I silenced the arguments developing in my head
I never said another word to her
but between you and me
all that perfume and arrogance aside
I know I could have taught her a thing or two
she could have learned something new about gender-bending
and multiple
orgasms
maybe she could have taught me things
about the way I've been coming
to terms with my own sexuality
but straight girls are often unwilling to make that slide
it cost too much to ride that wave for more than a wink
a feel
that feeling of power
now and then one might even dip her hand
all the way in to test the tide
and truth be told
most of us dykes enjoy the time of day they choose to give us
only in private do we confess to each other
that straight girls require too much effort
and stitches in groups larger than the accepted nine
and on that afternoon in question
I could neither afford the insults the expense nor the time

WHITE NOISE

The blast of the Q-train rushes in through the glass window
the thick pane holds fast against the onslaught of sound

New York apartments is always happening inside
police/fire/sirens/drivers blowing violent horns of ritual

in Baldwin's country
survival is to sleep through a crane knocking a hole
in the wall you used to call a view
dirty hands extend up from metal arms
silver teeth unearthing the roots a changing horizon

fat rats be running
rings of garbage and glory round the mesh cans
never enough of them
to house the milk cartons smiling with missing white children

here
I learn to tell you my life story in a play I made up
for real

in a studio
a small sink, a bathroom stall
I write poems on the side of the stove
and pretend to see a world no one else can

this place beckons the bizarre
the screeching, snaking trains, the dark tunnels
the blank faces begging outside the flagged windows

every day is a carnival here
the queer/the quick/the kind dressed in costumes
all of us belly dancing with Beelzebub

everybody brick-hard despite the quandary
of our common conundrum

New York: the place where everything screams loud enough
to create one big white noise

FIRST GREEN

Earmark me images
speckles pretty
with the tears of a child

open windows and summer
approaching
ominous air—marked with the first green

leaf
over-turned poems
forgotten
mouths tinkling humor

pages rustling
soft
sensible shoes
cushion/support/words

they unwind me
orange and gray laces

you/me entwined/separate
swirled
ice cream hinting the weather

may soon be
warmer

FALL SNAKING

The traffic snakes sluggish towards Goshen
fall is knocking at the folds of me
again
every year
it comes dragging the cruel winter behind it.

sometimes I think death would be easier
than watching August pull the bright blue
from the summer sky,

sleep seems the reasonable choice to make
when leaves need raking,
when aching is a way to feel.

I unravel in the face of this cold ruthless travel

the October highway grins
like a crescent moon
half empty and mocking
under a metallic light, night hardens everything;
the earth, the heart. The windows, opaque,
mirror nothing.

skin and posture shrivel, bunch,
break. September poems come more slowly
around the bend. It is hardest to give

when everything is going; strangers,
friends, familiar roads, suddenly desire
more. The gavel pounds

anxiety spidering up the small of backs.
Grim images of a reaper
creeping insistent towards the light.

under the brilliant heartache of these trees undressing
each boned finger is screaming,

nothing of this will last!

even when each branch of every shrub
is finally naked before God

even that too shall pass

SOME OF THE THINGS I BELIEVE

Imagination is the bridge
between the things we know for sure
and the things we need to believe
when our worlds become unbearable

but in this world of schoolboy bullets
biological warfare and kiddie porn
it takes guts to believe in any God
so I practice on believing in the smaller things
till I am able to make room for the rest

I begin with believing there's a Santa Claus
except I believe Saint Nicholas is a holiday transvestite
and I believe in monsters lurking under the bed
because they give our children something to conquer
before the world begins to conquer them

and contrary to popular belief
I believe Bert and Ernie are straight
believe they're just waiting for the right girls to come along
I believe bongs are pieces of art
I believe it's wrong to fart in an elevator
And get off at the next floor, I believe whore
is a word we created for women who liked fucking as much as
men

and I believe most lovers will lie to you eventually
and though I believe two wrongs don't ever make a right
—sometimes slashing his tires makes you feel better

I believe Pinky and the Brain are revolutionaries
because—*every night*—they try to take over the world
like them, I believe there will always be something to fight for
so I believe in the sounds my lover makes during sex

I believe in eating East Indian mangoes (and lesbians) from
     Montego Bay
I believe in believing every day
—and for as long as we can—I believe
we should believe in something we don't know for sure
acknowledge the range of possibilities
unlimited by what we see
move reality with imagination
we decide what our destinies will be

ON PROP 8 AND BEING IN JAMAICA

*May 26, 2009, San Francisco—The California Supreme Court, by a
6-1 vote, today rejected a constitutional challenge to Proposition 8,
an initiative measure adopted by the voters at the November 4, 2008
election that added a section to the California Constitution providing,
"Only marriage between a man and a woman is valid or recognized
in California."*

I

The emoticons inside my heart blink
bizarre

Jamaica has upgraded

bit by bit
we have chomped at the past
today
one laborite prime minister
one Leftist lesbian
and a white writer from a Black country
all reading from them memoir

under a tree
by the thunderous blue waters
everything feels like it could be solved
with the sway of the waves promising forgiveness

the way tings running it look like we cover more ground
than me ever did hope for
from Montego Bay
to America
and fast as me can leave this country
here comes the voices of South Africa

hold close my sisters

Cape Town look exactly like my Montego Bay
rich white folks
and more and more poor Blacks kept lowercase

I write the damn thing in capital letters
RACE IS ONE BIG RAAS LIE!

between my nose and my father's ankles
there is no difference between China and Africa
big populations/free trade
and souls willing to work for nothing

pity the fools who think they can win this war with theoretical
    discourse
bodies are exploding in places where there are no recording
    devices
people are bloating in waters that are not so clear
broadcast them on TV
sell them for monies that never really existed
cover my responsibility
make me think I was the only victim
watch the market fall
and call me when it's over

II

Jamaica and me dance by moonlight
only then will she open her lips when she kisses me
tongues with soft truths frighten her

she likes the hard push of things defined
bones
breath
bellies that deliver what they carry during gestation

such are the necessary conditions of bearing fruit
all else bleeds the slimy slick of miscarriage

clot me a solid palm
twist my arm and I will not bend

damn this inconsistent water breaking before time

I intend to be fully formed
Jamaica
and America are healing into the same ill-stitched scar
tar and feather the past
and you will find the future burning

III

I never really cared about being nobody's wife
but you done raised the hairs on me pussy
on me neck
this is one heck of a fuck/dick/conundrum you drumming up

America
I work too hard
quarrel too much with my own land to make this pass
unaddressed

California
I expected better of you
my children have as much claim to this kingdom of gluttony
as any man and woman who marry in a gambling house

sometimes I want to throw bottles like we used to do in Jamaica
block the roads and burn tires so the rich cannot move as easy on
    land
tear down the federal red tape that lines
the path to our love being legal

am I going to die
before you give me the right to see my woman as spouse
if she goes before me

is it not my duty to bury her

IV

between the Vincentian
the American
the Jamaican and the Texan

we drank two bottles of wine at the Ritz

I tried
to make light of the Black man who implied
I had stolen my own credit card
in my own country

I read the papers from afar and tried not to weep too much

V

It wasn't long before
one of us started hallucinating
screaming from the balcony

o ye of not enough fight
change is a matter of trial and error

I am whole
motherfucker
and I deserve my whole life/my whole being
I am alive and dancing
despite your spiteful prayers
despite your loud supplications to your narrow-minded Gods

the one I sometimes believe in
don't give an ass's hair
whether I marry your man or my woman

from this racist hotel in Jamaica

the road looks long
but not impassible

my resolve to press ahead
remains tightened by your refusal

this blow has reminded me
how connected all these wars are

my crotch is back in the saddle
head down I am gaining ground
walk careful motherfuckers
walk careful in your misguided fun
look left
look right
keep guard
because I won't be alone when I come

ONE QUESTION

All my life
I have been trying to answer one question:

how to chart battles without starting wars

long shot some say
to catch that kind of truth
place it where anyone can see

one day/clear/as morning
another afternoon
the damn thing black like molasses
often
the body of it is as thick as love
in moments
hard as revolution

one question:
how to fight fire with warmth

I am only human
a frail light among other lights
we all flicker
fail each other

forgiveness is the thread that will always link us

lover
mother
stranger

even them that despise me
will only possess me
if I do not find a kernel of letting it go

if I am to thrive
I must plant such a seed
water the thing/I must tend it like an unexpected child

I have to love it
regardless of its genesis

fruit of the poisoned tree is still fruit

my mother maintains my father raped her
what then does she do with me
breathing still
in defiance of her rejection

the prickly part of being an activist
is being a writer

how do you tell your side of the story
without telling your torturer's tale
to make the telling good
to make it true

you have to always ask
one question:

how do I toe the line?

time and time again/you will have to pull back your rage
engage the facts
lay out the acts of occurrence

fuck your own commitment to reverence
a balanced hand
a nuanced stroke of reportage

this is how you say what really happened
against your most basic inclination

rein in the urge to blast the motherfuckers

do not call them motherfuckers
if it is stone/call it stone
do not even allow for rock
or pebble
stone-cold the truth
be ruthless in your honesty

tell only what is necessary to propel the action forward
dust your petticoats off
stand firm in your platform of integrity

when all is said and done
let it not be whispered
that you were murky in your trust

one question should guide you

intention or honor
glory or gain
love or revolution

the options are all the same
in name or deed
the creed must be outside the realm of reproach

and if you fuck up
you pen your apologies
publicize them

print them on every page that will allow
follow your gut
the butt of all truths leads back to your middle

fiddle with your listening parts
tune in

thin the walls that separate you from yourself

find that one question
answer it

if you can
plan to spend your whole life
telling
not only the hardships you have endured
but also
the terror others have lived through

because of you

IN THOSE YEARS

BERNICE PERRY: THE DETAILS

My grandmother rises before the sun
alarms the morning with her hair almost white now
unfurling sturdy plaits of wisdom
thick and unrefined—like her philosophies
brushing the coils
separating the truths
until each wired strand is a filament
silver and Black reaching out to define the woman there
a moving chiaroscuro framed by the half-lit window

    that silhouette glides unfettered into morning

daylight streaks in
reveals the 117
perhaps 118 warts dancing circles
under her eyes
some with edges flattened and frayed
seasoned like Sunday clothes worn
for more than sixty years of *hallelujahs* and *amens*

some are new
itching with the rains
torrential like youth
she says I am my mother's child
mouth always open in defense
feet always light in the leaving

the numbers grow sparse toward the mouth
permanently pursed in prayer
for the children who left for North America and never came back
    she bears the scattered few
for the grandchildren too—dark bubbles of hot chocolate
floating in a milieu of broken promises
and severed umbilical cords

she believes in the crucified
still begins the day with a rosary of our names
Lord protect them,

Mavis/Howard/David/Blossom/Olga/Ann Marie/Delano/and
Staceyann

      arthritic knees bent
      she invokes our safety
right hand resting on the large print bible
one of them sent her from America

there is eighty-seven years of fat in her tale
the telling has made it soft in places
so she is comfortable
my head upon her belly cushioned in the sounds of
cornmeal porridge sweetened with condensed milk
she nurses a desire to see me full-figured
      winces when I walk by in tank tops
      dreams of me in shifts
      searches the nights for fish
swims toward the muddy waters; away from the clear
      for that is death
but moving gills promise life
and she wants the great grandchild
before she dies
      she begs me to take care
and *for God's sake eat something*!
      drink a mug of comfrey every day
and go to church once in a while

      she survives her battles daily
targets defined by round white tablets
softened with tap water twice a day
her gait is slow, precise
error seasoned by experience
she cooks curry without a recipe
and speaks truth without her hearing

I am still cracking Uzis at anything that moves

she is still laughing at me,
     when a trunk is still supple, she says
     the sap will make it bend
     she cackles and tells me,
when you have sacrificed entire branches to save a single leaf
     that would be time enough
     time enough, to call yourself a big woman tree

HAIKU FOR MY MOTHER

Chinaman left her
Black child in her flat belly
rock/stone in her heart

IN THOSE YEARS

If only out of vanity
I have wondered what kind of woman I will be
when I am well past the summer of my raging youth

will I still be raising revolutionary flags
and making impassioned speeches
that stir up anger in the hearts of psuedo-liberals
dressed in navy-blue conservative wear

in those years when I am grateful
I still have a good sturdy bladder
will I be more grateful for that
than for any forward movement in any current political cause

will I wish then that I had taken that job working at the bank
or the one to watch that old lady drool
all over her soft boiled eggs
as she tells me how she was a raving beauty in the sixties
how she could have had any man she wanted
but she chose the one least likely to succeed
and that's why when the son of a bitch died
she had to move into this place
because it was government subsidized

will I tell my young attendant
how slender I was then
paint for her pictures
of the young me more beautiful than I ever was
to make her forget the shriveled paper skin
the faint smell of urine that tends to linger
in places built especially for revolutionaries
whose causes have been won
or forgotten

will I still be lesbian then
or will the church or family finally convince me
to marry some man with a smaller dick
than the one my woman uses to afford me
violent and multiple orgasms

will the staff humor my eccentricities to my face
but laugh at me in private
saying she must have been something in her day

most days I don't know what I will be like then
but every day—I know what I want to be now

I want to be that voice that makes
patriarchal preacher-types
so scared they hire some butch Black bodyguards

I want to write the poem
that the New York Times cannot print
because it might start some kind of Black or lesbian
or even a white revolution

I want to be forty years old
and weigh three hundred
and ride a motorcycle in the wintertime

I want to be the girl your parents will use
as a bad example of a lady
the dyke who likes to fuck men
the politician who never lies
I want to be that girl who never cries

I want to go down in history
in a chapter marked miscellaneous
because the writers could find
no other way to categorize me

in this world where classification is key
I want to erase the straight lines
so I can be me

MY GRANDMOTHER'S TONGUE

She gets shorter every year
her ninetieth birthday bending her into a new century

now
she has the time to wonder
how the seeds of her womb
have come to such silence

hearing is hard for her
      the twilight taxes the organs of the poor
great–grandmother
      she wonders if the children born in exile
      look anything like her

American residents,
their visits infrequent and few
they bring too many sweets anyway
old people should not partake of such pleasures
dying flesh cannot withstand it

I don't know the names
of the grandchildren in Europe
I have buried the umbilical cords
that connect me to their future
the past lies trapped beneath my tongue
my children have taken their children
out of my house and I can no longer hear them. . .

This is what I imagine she would say
if she had the painted words
prodigal that I am
the daughter of a different land
America has opened its hand

and I am no longer drawn to the place
that birthed me

wood floors have hardened
to concrete structures stretching
high above my mother's mother's aspirations

my grandmother has become a ritual of memory
and I am hard-pressed to translate
her dialect communicates necessity

      Another woman warms my bed

my mother speaks
French phrases in Cologne
her German-Canadian child has never heard
Jamaicans sliding their tongues over the blunt patois
she only dreams of America—home of the faded blue jeans
pale skin and long fingers like mine
oxtails and boiled bananas are foreign to her

grandma can hardly see anymore
the night falls more quickly for her
familiar words in her mouth reassure her
she mutters Biblical names over and over and over again
impossible to learn new ones
      trust in the Lord and be of Good courage
      she knows the words of her salvation
foreign names are unnecessary
and how would she say Larah Frederica Hayle Mills-Moller
Diamonique and Sherrell are out of reach

Lisa
might have been possible
but Munich is a lifetime away
and her tenure is close to being over

FEELING UNFAMILIAR

My place among this generation of voices is lost

I can no longer hear my own blood pounding in my own ear
I am not even sure I am still alive
among these millions of poets pulling rhymes out their asses
without washing their hands

I watch them greet strangers

eat meat with them
as if I were never vegetarian
having learned to tear the flesh of things bleeding from the bone
nothing of me is recognizable to a self once so assured of purpose

I am still childless
and Africa grows big under my ribs
at night children from Uganda indict me in ebonics
in my dreams
Jamaica calls with foreign notes of birds I used to know
        grass quit
        hoppen dick
        cling-cling
I have not seen a pattooh in years
tears do not come easily to me anymore

feeling is unfamiliar
and if I were really being honest
I would confess that I watch way too much cable TV
to be really critical of the American media

I am torn between being Black
and being supported by a white gay audience
after so many years of being exotic

I am tired of having an accent
tired of acting like I know this woman I have become

I am longer certain of what
in this heart beats honest anymore
eons ago I was a lightning rod striking anywhere the iron was hot
today my exposed breasts lay frozen under the lights
truth is with parts of Black America in my mouth
I am no longer foreign enough
to say anything radical and get away with it
And in this PC climate
everything is a fucking compromise

so I have to be careful
of what I say about these young dykes
acting like getting some dick is revolutionary
like acting like a dick is revolutionary
like hating the vagina is progressive
like calling me woman is an insult

I am so angry at you
for not seeing how that behavior apes the culture that is used
to funnel Black boys into the prison industry

I am so angry at myself
for not having the words to tell you
how beautiful you are when you are not trying to be so
        invulnerable
I want to drag you neck and collar into a room
ask how you can so lightly turn away
from the politics that gave you the right
to have a fucking opinion?

but this poem is about my failings not yours
you are still young enough to correct your wrongs
still supple enough to bend the winds of progress toward a world
that better houses all the identities you desire

never mind that identity politics
is really a Jamaican–Chinese–lesbian–girl
writing poems about living out a chosen exile in America
that shit is so old and tired/I am so tired of crossing borders
and crashing into a self that used to be more fearless

I am really beating myself here
how's that for a sexual metaphor?
for a generation that thinks fucking itself into a drugged stupor is
    new
you all need to check the footnotes on the nineteen sixties
everything about pussies and asses
and dicks has been done and done and done

and I am just about overcome with the sadness
of Africa
the overheating environment
how my own humanity has become
a hard stone
sinking lead under the weight of how much I need these young
people
to put their fucking identity politics on pause
and give me a hand up out of this bloody depression

NEIGHBORS: FOR CENTURIES

In the past we sat
softening your pale hands
on porches and verandahs
squinting our tired eyes
so we could better watch your horizon for rain
even as the same sperm traveled up the brutal canal of knowing
you pretended the growing mulatto child
was conceived another way
both of us
his property
swallowed the violation and bled our pain away

our cycles
must have synchronized our wombs
cocooned as we were
in those small rooms shared by the birthing
the stained sheets pulled from under your cushioned legs
were used to wipe our blood from the wooden floor
we were both whores in the same brothel
you just had a better bed

anyone can trace our veined connection
across the skies of our raped histories
the mystery of how we both bore the affront
is still evident in the way you do not know
why my hair does what it does
when it has not been butchered
or lye-d
or pulled straight by the heat of iron hands

            centuries later
            we are still walking out of step
            with our documented conscience
every day we silence our need for vengeance

for solidarity with you
we stifle the scent of our rising moons
to raise your sons in safety

do you know
we scalped our daughters to be accepted by you

the sting still lingers in the way
Black women are offended by the convicted afro
on my sleeve
I do not believe we have to be separate
but equality should be more than a dirty word
frat girls use in college essays
for extra credit
I am saying
there is a deficit
in the fine balance of our feminine frailties
I am saying
the women's movement has always made use
of my dark body
in the marching
and the flag making and the taking of references
when it needed it
the statistics line themselves up
as columns twisting my spine
it is time we stood up
to be numbered among those wanting retribution
the extent of our contribution demands
that we be given some consideration
in the distribution of wealth
and health insurance policies that cover therapy
we would like to have someone to look at the wounds
we have been stitching
            for centuries

we have been fighting for this
            for centuries

and we are tired
and angry and entitled and hungry
we are also flesh
and breath and beauty
the forgotten duty of the sisterhood
we are bone and broken
and bleeding and needing to be heard

I do not wish for you
        to relinquish privilege
but the definition of the word
privilege must
widen
include the hand of every woman
whose lips were made thinner by the knife of religion
        the concerns presented
        must be representative of the collective
our politics must ground itself
in more than the wishes of the favored few
        none of this is novel to you
these conditions are absolute
and necessary
and non-negotiable
and long overdue
you have to hear us
see us
white woman you have to speak to us soon
else you might have the colored girls
guerrilla resisting
in a new a war against you

ELSEWHERE

Tonight I want to be elsewhere
more so in that warm place
pulsing with the temper of my people
they understand my snap-elastic words
collapsed into the undulating heart of a rapid dialect
broken down to expose the memory of a stone love blues
and a dawta rocking steady in a blood-red pum pum shorts
worn only under the heat of a Jamaican December

I loathe the lilt of my acquired accent
and though I still say *schedule*
when I speak of being in Everette
or Adrian or Tiffin on Tuesday
it is difficult to remain honest
because some people will never believe
anything you say

a girl in Wenatchee, Washington
tells me I fuck women by choice
Black mothers need to pray more for their Black sons
she said
racism is a choice the victim makes
and God will do everything to save us

God will always send his anointed to touch the unprotected

when I was exactly fourteen years and two months old
a preacher man told me I had glorious breasts for a body that small
young Black girl that I was
I was flattered by his attentions
might have had sex with him
if his mouth did not smell like feet

and it's funny
how we grow out of things like that in a foreign country
lovers need only be breathing
the older we get

the more grateful we are for the lone phone call
from Atlanta
or Austria
inside the dark of this America
a faraway voice can sound like a window
and if you say it just right
New York becomes a prayer
for those who need to belong to somewhere
anywhere is better than here
where the dialects merge soft into one another
like the dark flesh we label inferior

under the cruel tongue of an unforgiving fire
I walk softer in strange places
my body disguised in Texas
in Washington DC
nobody recognizes me in Cincinnati
I could be anyone in Cleveland
just another body in the line-up
strange bitch with the funny accent
I'm just another immigrant
on the run
been moving so long
my feet don't need direction anymore
just another night
another immigrant
wishing I was someplace that spills
the warm tears of my people
they understand my words
without the need for the cool
apologetic
and too often
imprecise translation

WAR GAMES

For Christopher Conti

1. Allegiance

In the fall of 1990
I let go of my virginity
The Desert Storm blasting loud from his 13-inch TV
of course it was summer there
Kingston sweltering
sweat collecting in my navel trembling
in the face of the unknown

I wondered then
if the explosions were for me
or the little people on the blue screen
far away from my pleasure
they were pictured small
boys with metal rods pointing to where they suspect America
might be

today I make love to a girl
the sound of this New War everywhere
wonder what we will lose this time

this time
I was visiting
home for when it began
bright
silver bombs bursting clouds
buildings
the victims
everything looks small on cable TV

I don't know
maybe the boys in Kuwait lived

maybe only their dreams died in the gulf that year

but I will never be that girl again
slow turning beneath his hands

I am a woman now

2. Flags

my little brother walks home with a kid from Afghanistan
my brother doesn't know
what the kid from Afghanistan thinks about the war
but everyone knows he has family at home
he knows he likes the Mets more
than he likes the Yankees

I'm not sure what kind of passport he has
but they both go to Brian Piccolo School/IS-53
and he likes being a freshman there

this war will take years
we are told
nothing more concerns us
we are told

these boys will be men when it is over

LOVE

WOMEN OF COLOR

Somewhere between midnight

and the hours after
I cough/rasp
exhausted

conversations of race/class/privilege
in a house called

women of color
a spectrum of shades/not white

women of color
collapse me/differentiate me

from white women
collapse us/Latina/brown/Black/Chinese is just one kind of Asian

call it what it is
women of color/women not white/women without the privilege
of health insurance/livable wage/the room to study and preen
without judgment

to walk through any neighborhood/safe

life taps at me
bloody

tonight I bled
and had to scavenge for a product

tagged feminine hygiene/as if my cunt is filthy
for breeding

just a bit of blood
a few days of bleeding

and I can give you a son
a daughter

if I was inclined to lay down for you
I might
in these days I ache for a child

but I do not walk/lie/writhe that route anymore
dyke that I am
I will make my own child

bleed for myself
for a woman of color/maybe

I bleed for all these little girls
under siege because they are not white

some white girls be of color too
not white enough/for being poor
or fat or squat or you ain't talk the right way to be white

these labels hang heavier than the chains that bind them
around us
and poor white girls

bodies labeled as trash
disposable

of color
not white

tonight this body is drowning in flu/blood/fatigue
frustration

everything makes my body hurt
especially missing you

parts of me scattered all over this country
my poems
half in love with everybody

but my hands
my heart is mostly in love with myself
with this girl of color
this Jamaican girl/not white

night colored/under some lights
I read as not so dark

but put my ass in a park with some real white folks
and I am as Black as they come

till I speak out loud
with more than my hands

then that Queen's English rolling comfortable
off my tongue
spills my body into owning places

because I am Black
I walk less Asian

invisible Chinese girl
Jamaican tongue

slim/bitch/stitching parts of a broken identity together

in Connecticut
two times in six days

in one week

I have spoken at Yale
Wesleyan/New Haven/Middleton

late night
hotel whispers with old lovers

new friends
I am learning
the sound of breaths not my own

the last time I was here
I held your face
familiar/new/you smelled like the other woman still

I held you
and you kissed me
one last time

and it was enough
that you came

closure they call it closure
women of color rarely get closure

more often/we bleed/untended
invisible

in houses named for us
we mark lines in the sand

pretend these boundaries
protect us

inclusive/the term
collapses me/you/us/into everybody

the features/melding/one giant woman

of color/a woman/not white

pretty woman/I dream about making love to you
all day
I press your words close to my tongue

I dare not say the name of the woman
of color walking Black between worlds

I move real/stealthy
pressed close to my Blackness

my heart opens
wide and of color

red/blood/pulse/breath

where are you now?

late night/woman
do you ever think of me
after hours

after midnight/do you still think of me
sprawled coral cross your body of color

woman
late/night/sick and bleeding

I am thinking of you

burrowed
north of the city/somewhere

and every poem
is always a love poem

no matter
what the inclination

shades of brown/removed

I am aching for one of you
the preference is unclear

after hours
every/body lives in shadow

the soft
dark/covering skin/thin veil of color

borrowed
burrowed

and I am in Connecticut
dreaming in shades of you

CATCHING MYSELF

Twice this week
I have caught myself muttering/mumbling/praying
for babies I have never met

have only seen/on TV
in airports/children I have taught
once or twice

my pen is angry at how much I do not know
about mothering
the miles and miles I do not want to go
by myself

the stories I am yet to hear/the salt tears

I will have to wash myself seven times over
dip me river after river I will administer ablutions

break my skin
thin my own blood trying to make space
for the things I must remember

I am exhausted by the worry
the waiting/the watching of lives seeping by

red and yellow
black and white
they are precious in his sight

I suppose that rhyme
once meant something

in another life/I believed

belonged to something bigger than my own inclinations
gone are the days
when preachers/and parishioners
prescribed my prejudices

I am in love with my own laughter
my hands rove my own body

my story
is my own/to give to whomever I choose

whose approval do I seek now?

a lover is required
to love me

imagine me beautiful

novel intention/to desire a woman
who does not pick at you

your flesh decaying under her criticism

mothers/daughters/sisters
grandmothers/aunts

the X-chromosome is socialized
to tear at itself/at others like itself

consume the softer parts of a palm outstretched

affirmation given
woman to woman is rare

between these walls where girls live
we are expected to pull/push
give birth to hard things

and when it emerges
without compassion

we are forced to survive it

twice today
I have held my stomach

stuttered a prayer for a child
I keep asking a God I am not sure I believe in

to send me something
alive

and breathing

please/God/don't make me stop bleeding
without the fruit of my own womb

and some days
I can see your little face
willing me to come get you

only problem is I'm not sure
exactly what you will do to the warrior in me
will you calm my waters

pour oil on the rougher parts of me
will you make me quiet

passive
I do so love this fight I keep trying to put down for you

for you I would do anything
but that

how can I hold your countenance
alongside all the other faces I keep dreaming in horror?

how can I be soft enough
to keep you nestled/and remain the sharp dagger
I have been nursing for years

these fears keep me from you
every year
I postpone your arrival

these harsh words in my mouth/these dreadful truths
of girls trafficked
raped
bodies skewered on the stake of our politician's ambitions

boys charred brutally into men
lies told effortlessly to babies

how do I beckon you here
knowing the terrors that await you

love is sometimes not enough to keep a child/safe

often
our intent
falls short of its target

choke-holding the victims/clueless in its cruelty

how many of us
were bystanders in our parents' war
far and wide spans of geography/time/generations

we bear the ugly marks of knives dragged serrated across our skin
in vain/we beg our father to apologize

our mothers are yet to admit there was ever
any foul play

anything that happened/not saying that anything did
but if there was any tragedy
you draped it over yourself

no one wants to be accountable to some thirty-year-old memory

an imagined sin cannot be forgiven by a God you cannot trust
so you keep your counsel/bite your lips/for fear of being labeled

the mad woman in the attic

you rock your old wounds to sleep
suffer the childish recollections

speak no evil/because no one want to hear/of such evils

years later
you are huddled in a room
in South Beach/reaching for an answer you know
that will not come

how do I numb myself/enough
to bear a child/wild enough to survive me
and my nights/my terrors/swishing salt like an ocean

how do I not drown in these truths I have written
in a book
I wish I could take back

I am trying not to count the ones I will lose/trying to

keep track of the ones who promise to stay
the numbers who will follow the lines you wrote/and nod

the ones who will make art of your telling
the ones who encourage you
to love a child enough to birth it

bear your truth/child/they say/bear your truth/carry it
honestly
and maybe
if you are honest enough

your own flesh will replicate
and the fruit of it
will flower/bloom

become more than this hesitant/unfinished prayer
the coward in you
keeps postponing

ZURI-SIALE SAMANYA

Her name
means vulnerable/resilient
rock of beauty/reason for love

I wanted her name
to echo the warrior women
who came ahead of her/ahead of me
Madonnas/whores/mad women in attics
virgins who were never really virgins
except when they needed to be
smart women

make your own list of saints
my daughter/fondle it often

this rosary of Amazonian nomenclature

my own mother left early
left me inside a closed fist of unforgiving women
who never expected me to ripen well
the apple never fall far
watch that tree/it will come to no fruit

but look at you/daughter
shiny/red/apple/tomato/baby/it is my intention to be
different/with you

I can hardly wait
to hear your voice
I expect us to rumble
to create generational bruises that will have to be survived

forgive me/daughter/for the sins I know
will stain your childhood

send you to some stranger's expensive couch
to thrash out how your mother
never loved you/loved you too much

I hope we will be able to breathe through it
not unlike the way I breathed through your coming

oxygen mask over mouth
I mumbled the list of saints I keep ready
Audre Lorde
Adrienne Rich
June Jordan
I called for Pat Parker
for my grandmother/Bernice
your heart pulsed wild then
rapid dance forcing them
to slice me open

and then/suddenly/ you were here
wide-eyed and alert/you surveyed the damage
and did not blink
I remember thinking
this shit should come with a fucking manual
somebody should be telling me what to do

my Brooklyn apartment is too small for two people
two people/God!
I'm people now/two people
two mouths to feed/two asses to wipe
two bodies to keep safe
two of everything/needed/schizophrenic existence
Dear God, what do I do/now? What do I do/now?
What the fuck do I do now?

FOR YOU

Round and about the edge of things

seasons
books
loves
truths

and other follies
follow my palm

divine
lies and wonder

work and wells dug with the bones of broken vows

nothing is meant to last
move too fast and the fury will come
brutal

slow killing on a floor designed for breaking things

hearts
knees
chains

cryptic like dust sprinkled on the grave of an enemy
write me poems

build me pillars
you will eventually tear them down

weep
whirl
wonder what happened

what happened to that small girl
gentle like rain

clean water from the tropics
none of this acid falling from these harsh skies

come back to me
my Jamaica

simple
like racism is just prejudice in shades
easy
like tripping was only over a rock

dock me two days pay for not showing up
not like this kiss-me-arse reality where they does fire you
for asking permission
to be absent
to be free of these cubic rooms

these desks nailed to white walls of forever

eternity is a long raas time
grime or palace
my toes like to be done

once a week
at least

I like a massage
it frees the shoulders for dancing
the legs for running towards things

my mother has been absent from my phone for months now

no answer
no way to tell if she alive or deathly afraid of living somewhere

anywhere I turn
I am so frightened of becoming my mother

lonely old woman
no bells to speak of
only the memory of what she never did right
tolling
tolling

for her
for me

for her three children
oceans between me
and the boy I first adored/brother

Grandma has been dead two years and some
today the rain came in sheets

gray glimmer glaring angry at New York

this town is not for the lonely
or only for the lonely

sad
sad
the wing of October falls
cold
cold

mutinous my muscles refuse to move
what good is dancing
when the heart lies still
beneath the earth of things suffered

sometimes survival
is not good enough

wear me
thin girl
loud girl

pin me on your chest

display me
clay and dust

I am only human

flailing
failing
falling

fleeing
who am I fooling
if you come for me

I will follow you anywhere

false are these furrows
these furies

these flippant
ferocities

for you
I would fold
freely

feel the fetters float away
for you
I would follow all the follies

for you
I would
I would

RAISE THE ROOF

White supremacy must be in the water
ingested by police/the prosecutor
and the politicians
who remain silent while a steady staccato of Black bodies
fall like leaves/in Ferguson/in Cleveland

It is autumn in America
and the world has lost its fucking mind
white cops caught killing on camera
forcing us to relive the constant killing of our kin
—a new story cracks our consciousness/every day
every day we watch/those viral videos
becoming more and more numb/more struck dumb
by the sheer gall of these cops steady snuffing out
Black lives in their made-in-America home movies

every day I have to drown my fears
for my child/born Black and girl in a country
in which her safety does not matter
to anyone with any power

I try not to think about
—the catcalls in her future
—the crass comments Black boys make
about Black girl bodies—but this poem is not about that
this poem is about the blatant racism
embedded in the national justice system
it's about Grand Juries
that consistently refuse to indict murderers
captured on video/it's about the consensus of white opinions
that overwhelm the evidence
available to anyone with a fucking cellular phone

I am consuming these murders/on repeat

the helpless bile rising angry in my chest
public shootings/documented/by onlookers
images passed around after the event
this phenomenon is Black lynching two point O
except this time we are spectators of our own genocide

consuming the flesh of these murdered women and men
who were never willing martyrs in our movement
dead children of parents who now mourn them
without closure/without a day in court
we are moving backward through history
back to that time when Black mothers
who lost children to white arrogance had no recourse
that shameful time/that supposedly ended
with Emmett Till
with Herbert Lee
with Medgar Evers
with Harriette Moore
with Malcolm X
—back then/there was no hypocrisy about
the system being stacked against anyone
with a smidgen of melanin staining the history of their skin

five decades after the Black civil rights movement
and we are still not protected by the law
this is not what we voted for
when we voted our first Black president
this is not what our freedom fighters hoped for
when they marched against segregation in Selma
and Chicago and Birmingham and Montgomery
this is not the dream Dr. Martin Luther King died for
in Memphis, Tennessee

fifty years later/race relations in America
is still a fucking cauldron bubbling angry
under the ugly swirl of Black despair
held in place by the lack of white accountability

parading as a penal system/in which
forty percent of those incarcerated
come from a group which only consists of 12 percent
of the entire fucking population

with numbers like that
what good does it do me
to comply with those in uniform?

body riddled by forty-one bullets
for raising your hands while holding a candy bar
shot-dead at twelve for holding a toy gun
strangled by an illegal choke hold/for selling loose cigarettes
arrested without cause/for walking and talking while Black
all this while we pay taxes
and vote for white presidents
presiding over these United States
as if Black death did not matter

this country continues to default
on the promise of citizenship for Black people

—a system sworn to protect us
owes us something when it fails
a system sworn to protect us
owes us something when it fails

in the roll call for protection
all Black bodies must be accounted for
straight/queer/transgender
lesbian/feminist/Muslim/man
woman/immigrant/dark-skin/
non-binary/tall/fat/skinny/light-skinned
in the face of any killing
our sorrow must be one/our rage must one
though we speak with many voices
we must rise with one sound

we must call out the names of the dead
Trayvon Martin
Tamir Rice
Yvette Smith
Michael Brown
Kiwi Herring
Sean Bell
Tarika Wilson
Sandra Bland could have been any one of us

we have to find the fortitude to keep fighting
for ourselves
for our children
for our children's children
it is time to put our bodies where we say our politics lie
this is not a moment to invoke the sweet by and by
this is a moment for civil fucking disobedience
 no matter what you do to our flesh
no matter how long you wage war against our spirit
our bodies will remain a force of resistance
to the proliferation of White Supremacy
no matter where you came from
no matter how you got here
inside the brutal walls of these United States of America
white power must always meet fire when it meets with us

if there is any humanity left in you
get up
stand up
sit-in
join a fucking protest
pick up a fucking pen
write
scream
wail
march
pull down a fucking racist flag
plan

scheme
plot a way forward
fucking strategize
it's time to raise the roof on these motherfuckers
it is time for America to come to terms
with the permanent fact of Black bodies

you have to get used to us white people
make a decision to do right by us
do it willingly/or unwillingly
we don't fucking care
as for the progressive white liberals among us
find the words
to speak to the racist white relatives you keep disowning
all of you have got to get with the fucking program
because our Black asses are never/ever/ever going away

WHY I BE WRITING YOU POEMS

I be turning your picture

smiling upright now
warm showers are mine
you said and that made me tuck myself
deep inside these first chills of fall

It seems October will always be mine
a thing I would prefer shared

but what can I do
when I grow busier each day

driving
East New York and stillness
cousins
dinners eaten in solitude

learning the note of one
is hard
but I am softened
by the memory of soapy water and hotels

and how my take on this end
swings pendulum

these days
there is the rest you craved
and I am not quite so exhausted

even without sleep
I lounge inside myself, lazy
productive

please don't leave me
I begged
and you haven't
you pretty girl exquisite in slumber

I think of you
curled philodendron round my torso
not bitter tonight

I miss you
senseless caught between consciousness and dream
recall how it made me chuckle to ask you
favors in that half-wakened state

I miss you
four tiny minutes past midnight
no desperation
just me and the quiet hurt of you absent
just me immobile and breathing

I think of you among friends
your grandmother's new voice stirring understanding
loyalties reconfigured to widen theories

include feelings

I am glad you shared them with me
was grateful for the chances
we seem to have earned
in a past life we must have been sisters
before that mother
or daughter
or both

friend is the one that needs work in this lifetime
you said
and I am learning to hear you
static I am twisting the nob to listen with both hands

ears cocked
my whole chest belongs to everything I have feared
and I am taking it back

your feet
my face
our friendship
soft like we made love

our words look like lips
tongues
teeth tugging gentle in play

you are the only woman I have ever trusted
with a flame
perpendicular to my heart
the scent of melting candle heady on my belly
my back
my legs will always lead me compass
to you
your truths
and the way you move me even now

far and away
fairy tales fading reality still grabs me knuckle
in my gut turning
stories
grandmothers
babies
sisters and how we worry about them

don't leave me, again, I beg me to stay

even when the tides crash uncertain against me
under you

beneath us the ground shifts water

sand
we have to trust there is rock

you are my Jamaica
wrong or right
sanctioned or disdained

I am learning to love us each
separate
tearing in parts

but somehow
remaining whole

FAST AS I NEED TO

I am about to teach myself
To fly slip slide flip run
Fast as I need to
On one leg

from June Jordan's "I guess it was
my destiny to live so long"

Having considered death I
suppose I
must have loved her

    the scorned quandary
    rests guilty on my chest cracking
    shoulders heaving apology
for having allowed the tempting yen
to flourish despite the carnal knowledge
of her mouth on another neck
less than two weeks after our dissolution

    in my foolish grieving I forgot
that heartbreak is a privilege
wrapped in kilos of fatty flesh sliced impolite
from the courage of women
surviving pink ribbons and chemotherapy

    such immaturity can only be excused as passion

    in my silent suicidal reverie I disremembered that
death is the Sisyphus of tragedy humanity is still attempting to
outrun

accept my regret for letting the hours pass
without words/without protest

without praise or gratitude to the lives who marched
        so this generation could execute the right to brood
            to bury myself safe
under the soft dark comfort of a New York apartment
            the wide windows covered
              the red and gold Ghanaian print of curtains
            weeping
        over recorded images of old brown legs
rotting toxic in rusting wheelchairs
rolling by on ticker-tape-fast/er than I could absorb

memory/desire
        and a fretful impending winter
mock my tragedy sniffing her remains
lingering cinnamon on my pillow/long after she left
        dark after dark after dark
        I slept between the musky sheets
ignored the flashing traffic
        the intermittent jolts of movement and light
        amidst the assault of passing cars and cable television
            I kept my eyes closed
        until June Jordan reached back
        pen and fury
        from the grave and roused me

    last poems
        pounding wit and ferocity she reminded me that heartbreak
is not an acceptable excuse for apathy

this war requires live bodies
to collect the dead
        the diabetic
        the teenagers
        the grandmothers
        the babies who are still alive are screaming
there will be time for adult wailing
        later

when we are done counting fingers and toes
found far from the homes in which
they may have curled in pleasure
            or pain

            once we have a number
there will be designated hours
for retching
and
and rebuilding the new New Orleans
that will no longer be for sturdy women
in sensible shoes
the blues they will play
will not be—no way siree
not for no poor Black people tap tap dancing bottle caps
rat tat tat on a brand new pavement

            we cannot yet spare one hand
in the necessary cavalry of resistance
            during the chipper discourse on the cost of rebuilding
            I wept for more than my own misfortune
the absence of your naked feet
seems insignificant in the foreground of this Herculean effort
to ingest this putrid un-Rwandan genocide
so forgive me
if I have put your leaving aside

forgive this forgetting of your flesh
before the appropriate time
            at the present juncture
such melancholia is a luxury

            furthermore
            death has already visited
and it would be inconsiderate of me
to extend so eager a welcome to it again so soon

ELEGY FOR PETER OF THE EARTH

In everything
let us recall that love is violent and fleeting
a thing into which all other things can be drowned

Arafat is dead and Sharon
flirts with him there. Other bodies tear
a folded heart, label it,
stomach
liver
pancreas
        a poet died last year
and in his final days
he needed no polishing
shiny as he was he glowed beacon into the next life

he left his lungs here
shrieking the lack of air
the television screams obscene
four hours a day in Europe

too many to count in America

tropical storms are hurricanes
trapped inside a limited dream
flail on little wind
these walls made of time could not hold you

the sky will wrap you cloud and light
sorrow and survival is how we must remember
the sweetened songs of a gentler afternoon

this Christmas will mark the first of winters
borne without you interrupting
your delicate hands blooming a pink flower
indecent like your mouth open in every photograph

poet
if you can see me
comb these lines for a truth
signifying our frail utterances

twirl us a new window from the old glasses you used to see
through
you always said
every experience must be paid in space
or distance/I told you not to forget the fees charged in blood

forgive us the necessary ruse of weeping
this losing of fluid everyday
it is just water we say only water

tell it like it is—like it is
you said/this is how it is

crazy cluttered
memories of things past
one more thing to reload elusive onto our screens
our tiny electronic spleens split to reveal the iron taste

this is the way we construct grief
one lifetime leaking
affluence into the darkest rivers while motherfuckers drown in
their own cunts
northern comforts passing blunts communal like dis-ease
rest with me here
Peter/Rock/steady *light/luz/licht*
point me toward understanding how you could leave us so quickly

faster than the speed of all things glowing
I am painting you red and orange and blue
the color of my love marks you permanent
perfect and twenty-nine
you had the gall to pass over one day before your thirtieth

you promised you would be here
for thirty you said thirty would mark you adult
erase the years between us
thirty-three would mark us both Christ .
direct you disciple or sinner or God

now I can only follow you
in memory
and wish
seven years
we were married seven years!

you gave me another life/*Another Country*
now death claims you immemorial
mirrors me widow—who would have thought me
widow/dyke

cancer/chemotherapy
quicksand/I miss you my friend/my fury
strikes me immobile
fiddle me an explanation of why you are not here
drinking the crimson wine I have only just learned to swallow

do you remember when I
could not weather the influence of spirits?
I never believed in Elegba
Oshun could kiss my ass/Christ was all I allowed you

say hello to these leaders/falling/statues
icons of a world imploding
building and bridges tumbling London
and New York
you wanted to see Tokyo
torrential like oceans flooding body and breath

your last moments were contained
I sat outside the small white room and prayed
for you I invoked heaven

for you Poet of the Earth/I spoke with a God
I was not quite sure existed/I bet my mutterings
on your beliefs
and lost
or so it seems from this end

tell me otherwise
poet send me a sign
a burning wind
some water parting/ a rock rolling up a hill of your choice
I need something to whet me/tune me into another world
turning tempered and timeless
come back to me/my blue/boy/girl
everybody has claimed you in death
you are conjured poet/singer/dancer of limericks unknown
sound me a sea/green lulled by the logic of you only sleeping
promise me I am only dreaming/promise
I am only dreaming you are gone. . .

MUTED GRATITUDE: FOR TRACY CHAPMAN

(After I saw her perform at Roseland)

You make me want to be a rock star

       I chose to be a poet
         because I had no abilities with the note
I stood neck deep in the dark sweat of women
screaming your name

muscled thick under black
too cool to dance
you just rock the crowd instead
moved white women to tears
and told a thousand nappy headed Black girls
that dread locks were the statement for sexy

that girlish smile on that face!
          I know that face!
the quick dip of the chin
the slow seep into a blush
your charcoal skin will never be dark enough to mask
the guilty pleasure of loving what you do

I have stretched my insecurities out under that smile
felt it's glow light up in the heat of my own revolution
on the face of a woman who loves sushi and salmon
I have kissed that smile into a giggle
it is the smile of a woman who likes the smell of herself
it is the smile of a woman who will touch your hair with her hands
and hold your sorrows with her heart

Like honey over the raw edge of leather
the forbidden urge of your voice cut

into the eager mouths of infants
dripped into the crevices of our flesh

the multitude swaying with want of
women in boxers
women in thongs—you could do no wrong in this crowd

you—with your strings
pulling our coiled insides from hiding
you—with your back
larger than they say it should be

woman I just wanted to be you

for one moment I wanted to touch the ball of soft night
you carry so light in your bosom
I wanted to lead my people out of the bliss
     of not knowing
     when not to lay down
     when not to take what life has offered
simply because they were born
in this country of thorns and roses

phoenix that you are
you made us rise to the sound of the gong
lift the ash from our heels and dance
swing our hips against the age-old slumber of silence
     and we shouted for you
     and for ourselves
     and for the selves we were still hoping to be

the battered women were jumping
the bashed lesbians were holding each other
each of us caught up in the frenzy

of the private-public conversation we were courting with you

we were drenched in the saga of you
water leaving your body like rain
music
leaving your fingers like fire

and you
making it seem like nothing
like being myself was all I would ever need to be

I wanted to thank you
       but you were gone
the empty stage
blinking it's wounded eye in a pulsating promise

With no other way to thank you
I simply folded my muted gratitude into myself
and used its dark ink
to write you a poem

TRINI GIRL

For Lynne

Trini girl
with your grandmother silence
twisted tight into the roots of your copper locks
      the follicle several shades darker than the tips
      wish you could tell me
exactly where the color hurts
      when the great light of mornings
      dark showers and see-through
      tears are not enough to hold you
together
      let me hold you
      sometimes
      let us
      mourn the loss of some lover or other
together
      be dazzling beyond the lyric of rhymes we turn
like tricks to convince each other
      we are surviving

      I know you are surviving

      I recognize the Toni gleam
in the slow pivot of emotion you carry in your mother's
mother's   indifference
spine ramrod   straight
backbone   upright and unending
body perfect   between   us

      I am grateful for the parallax
      of wet in your eye

my own vision is frequently   obscured
tears/island love song/the rescue/the constant

the cooing   hush girl—   everything go be alright
too often   you pull away   too fast
        but when you know my shoulders
have stopped   the heaving   the sloping
the need for things I have not learned to say

I wish you would stay longer
        sometimes
        wish I could ask how the night went
        or how you swallow the sorrow alone
        the clear uncertain saliva   rushing
        off your back

how do you stand the lack of warm
in your bed
        your white sheets stained
only with the scent of memory

wish I could ask you the questions
we seem to raise
        only in metaphors

but I have long learned to hold you
        close with clever knots of dyed
        hair tied into the known performance

I have accepted your grandmother's silence

I have learned to recognize the gleam
        in the tiny flash of light that no longer haunts me
        it just makes me want to hold you
        more now
        because I know you cry

INAUGURAL PRAISE SONG

For Elizabeth Alexander

Congratulations on a task
done with dignity
and pride/an unexpected consideration
of/for those we so often say we speak for/about

I am proud to know you/poet

press my hopes that those you love are close
safe
reveling in your accomplishments

days ago
the city turned
the nation
twisted itself a new skin

and you held your narrow rope
pulled our fraying parts together

socks
tires
pencils
all the tools were there

here's hoping we use them well/while the world watched/watches

say it plain
you said/say it plain

love is a sharp sparkle
a walk forward

a light
a song in praise for the poets

the people with purple fingers/reddened hands

the brick-layers/the threaders/the workers
the weavers of tales and cotton shirts
huddled and shuddering to survive our most brutal histories

you pulled us in
and warmed us
with a litany of our most necessary truths

I HAVE NEVER KNOWN WHAT WE ARE

un-mappable distance
denoting the divide between what time is it where you are
to no straight lines between who you are
and who I am always trying to be

intermittent
invisible I chart the wisps of things first said
things hinted at in subsequent/not quite had
conversations
snippets/of confessional detail
molded into a narrative I would tell myself

how many lovers/how many broken hearts
I have nursed/in between I would call you
sink stolen into the borrowed safety

you were always the woman
with the children
and now I am become
an insider to the task of motherhood
not quite the brood you birthed
but duty and desire has me equally wrapped

and I am unable to shake the fear
of how we could be stars
burning beautiful from afar
but brutally inadequate light

up close
we could be everything my ugly is afraid of

but here we are
moths to the flammable torch

of things uncertain
unexplained

In the past/in the fiction of my truest stories
I would write us forever
intertwined
weaving in and across the wild pulse of every so often

but something flickered
off/on
and here we are caught/deer in my own headlight
I am startled/uncertain
flailing under the new wash of colors

I feel naked
under your deliberate gaze
I am unsure I am deserving/still
I am asking

open-ended
there are no specifics to my question
only the blood red center it
stained with a desire enter your familiar
to have you walk freely through mine

I want to us to finally know the details

never mind that the heart of you
has always beat recognizable to me
no matter the perspective
cursory/skittish
I could always see
my most human errors/in your eyes
inside my best self/you were always love
fierce/unconditional
I required nothing/to love you
Gypsy/what I felt had no geography

no name/no borders
to make it big or small
it only was

truth or fallacy
I am advocating for the chance to see
why/how/who we could become
given the hours
to languish unhurried between pages of a story
not written in haste
not discarded in fear

prophetic
or foolishly fictitious
I am presuming that/that we are still etching
is in itself testament
of all there is left
to write

WHAT WE LONG FOR

I have never been sure of you

hook/line and heritage
of being Caribbean/born
to a mother who fly/off to North America
leave chile/with granny
granny do her best
but best believe/there were deficits

but this poem is not about things gone
missing/this poem
is about knowing/about love
and its impossible frailties

and in the face of our unfinished unfolding
who can claim such cocksure cognizance?

our love is like New York winters/blizzards
one year/not even a flurry the next
all the while/Mercury rising
and nobody feeling no heat
everybody watching their breath
freeze/nothing moving/except the hot horror
of one lascivious summer/sweating nasty
like the way we always fuck/and leave floods
and fires everybody still putting out
years later/we still sorting rubble/still getting in trouble
for inhaling things we should have washed
from both our hands

if this weren't real life
I could write us linear/like a Hollywood flick
craft every character fabulous/forever/after
if this were fantasy I could

forget the convoluted plot of us
here now/gone tomorrow

and there I go talking about things missing again
hard to stay in the present/when you ain't know nothing
but the past lasting longer than it should

only thing we could stand on is the rock of our beginning
cosmic love/riddled with rue
not unlike your most recent happenings
unfortunate
events breaking more things than we can count
on one hand

we always learn from such splintering
such regret
and I am stranded/somewhere between
understanding
and screaming/I can't fucking believe you
grand/fucking mess you have here
hurt hollowing out heartbreaks like it's Halloween
complete with grim reaper swinging that scythe/circular
heads rolling on bathroom floors

me

I'm steady/changing diapers
and singing lullabies
no lies between us
but this truth ain't no easy balm
blood and water/rock and time
you will always be
almost mine
yen is the word that best defines us
this unquenchable longing
makes it hard
to pen us

plus the fear of rejection
keeps my ass seated in the right aisle
no risk of being told
I'm in the wrong/place/my battle is against my own insecurities
my version of this narrative places me
behind everybody
but Pittsburgh/that old steel town
with nothing to be jealous of
but your memory of the Cheesecake Factory
the gray rain
and unimportant things left there

I am tired of our regret
returning year after year

today I am only sorry
we don't live the norm of most romances
mid-week lunches
overnight bags
and unexpected arrivals

I wish you could/come get me
today/after work/before twilight
between meetings/come fuck me
come right out/ask me/your place or mine
crime or punishment
I wish you would just decide to come
for me/to me

across waters and narratives
through history and hurt feelings
against the odds I wish you would come/claim me
publicly/tell the world how much magic we be making
when we make love
how we move mountains/cliché like love songs
sound/tracking/our movements
epic/like lovers/leaping/uncaring

from rocks/over/seas
drowning in our belief in the frail/impossibility
of love/and ending/happy
like fairy tales in anime
surviving/dragons and distance
and time

forever is a long time to love somebody
from afar/our current close-up reveals
we are more flawed than we feared
having bared more than we wanted to admit
we find ourselves/wanting/more

more songs/more long walks
more evenings/more early mornings
more fucking/more spooning
and still more/forks in the road/keep us hesitant
waiting for what-the-fuck/I-don't-know
we may just be
missing the point of all this epic/learning
Black cats/continually/crossing each other
parallel lines/never the twain shall meet
mathematical/impossibility

it's time one of us folded or changed direction

fate/or futility/truth or dare
it's time to piss
or peal your pussy/off the proverbial pot
longing is only sexy for a few lifetimes
after that it's just frustration/threatening to fling
everybody/over a fucking cliff

even this/poem is tired of its own longing

this poem needs action
this poem needs our follow through

this poem is about everything that haunts us
it's about small islands and big cities
it's about water/bridges and absolution
it's about forgiveness
handed over without restraint

this poem is about reaching out
and touching flesh
it's about holding space
and going all the way
this poem
is about you
and about me
and the long legacy of risks
we keep refusing to fucking take

FUCK WHAT YOU HEARD
ABOUT FALLING

Fuck what you heard about falling

love
is not for hearts that cannot survive breaking

let someone in
and you are bound to both trip over yourselves
crack some vital organ or other

the trick is
you must remain open for the healing
then
allow for a second fracture
a third

maybe even a fourth will be necessary
before you can call it
love
is about endurance
it is a journey of distance
and time spent getting to see what lies
resting beneath the veneer of the first pretense

those beginning days
are only the invitation/inked in gold letters
embossed with the hope of all things possible

that first intoxication is as sweet as first-light pussy

just before the sun stirs
before the hard edge of the day
has cursed you into caution
these are the hours of open palms

drawn butter-warm across pebbled nipples
crass innuendoes delivered in the tenderest moments

all this performed
your knee nestled between her thighs
your tongue lodged deep inside her cheek

such are the easy days of eating sugar
and fucking in the raw
in the splendor of the duck and covering
everything is easy to say
because nobody is saying too much

except the same song always
playing naive inside every cupid-infested head

nothing I don't love about you/baby
you are perfect for me
behind these flower printed glasses
you are just the right shade of everything I always wanted
a dream/become exactly what I have wished for
flesh forming around my fantasy

fuck what you were before I found you

you and I
don't need to table the time allotted
for mortals/our connection is cosmic
I know your thought before you think it

in fact
I don't need to think too much about what we are doing
having lived these lives before
no surprises ahead for us

such is the bullshit we have been ingesting
about commitment and the cost

of being vulnerable to someone you really know
over time
of hard tasks/completed in concert

someone who has broken your heart
more than once
is someone who already knows
what you look like when you are weeping
the way she knows
what you look like after you've farted/in a crowd
loud and shameful/she will stand by you
when the narrowed eyes/the flared nostrils
point accusing at your rear

you will know
why she trembles when her father calls
why she lies/about what she does/every day
to make her mother proud of who she isn't

true love is about knowing the worst
of what no else one knows
and still deciding she is amazing

done right/love has few rules

if you stumble
always
I should try to catch you
my arms will at least reach for you tumbling from the sky

love is never asking why I fell
when you know I do not yet have the words to answer
love is knowing you will forgive me
if I ask anyways

and when my human hands are not quick enough
to break your rapid descent

you will recall the times I caught you before
nose spiraling
down the stairs I warned you never to run

love is not a measure
of how much you can take before your courage snaps
love
is holding fierce
in the face of falling to pieces
over and over and over again
and having the faith to forgive
and still find laughter
almond milk shooting through nose/diving
down the length of her giggling

three years later
you should still want to hold her
fourteen days gone traipsing through the politics of Cuba
you should still miss her scent
night passing like some sloth dragging slow
the hands of every clock not moving fast enough for her return

the bloody bed too big for only you
and this ache for her ass pushed snug into your crotch on fire
for her

and you angry
that you could need anyone this much/that you let anyone
know this much about you
and not send her sailing
out some window of constructed glass

love is not knowing when you decided
you would stay/even though she isn't perfect
because flawed as you are
you both fit
bit by bit you are unveiling
strip/teasing

telling truths you never knew could be uttered
out loud
during sex
in the shower
at the dinner table
the power of love
lies not in the proud peacock prance
of the too often
dishonest courtship
but in the gritty survival of time
held over teeth
lasting through harsh tongues
and tears of glee
years and years and years of living
inside a reality where the falling
is not always
free

RACE TO THE WATER

Low/low down
under what we call intellect
there is a fire
I want it to turn up
not high enough to burn you
just to get you yearning

you have to trust it/thrust it

where there is flame
there must be water
so let/bubble/come through the rubble
of things we accumulate
things we learn to hate
eventually/it must begin
rising/racing/pushing at the edge
in the end
it must wedge you
betwixt and between the things
you have not yet discovered
let it carry you and me
over the river/wash us down
lift us out of this thrashing life
we want out of the gathering
of rat on top of rat

Race me to the water

Down/down
to the washer woman
the runner man
let in everybody
even the smallest child
disguised as muck/as bad luck

you cannot assume it
you have to watch it
catch it in your hands
feet and head spinning
you have to let it
pin you to the wire
you have to let it loose
lose your inhibitions
we are already everything we want
nothing we desire
is beyond us
even in these muddy waters
calling me back
ragged and whole
I am moving out of this slick slumber
urge me a humbler place
race me
walk me/carry me
make me run

take me
down to the water
into the water
over the wet
fret me a tune
make it bloom/loom like
weave it/trickle it threadlike
spike it
mike it
run it
one time
two time
all of your lifetime

LONG DISTANCE LOVE

Living in a place like New York
can be lonely for the traveler
who is really a poet
peddling politics for progress

add one small miracle/six months old
and crawling
and the scene is set for drama

life on the stage is no small feat for a new mother
add the lesbian bit
and the shit gets more interesting

everyday is about holding balance
your stance has to be sure
but ready to shift
if that's the shuffle needed
for packing pureed peas
and breastfeeding
for making your flight
and making new poems
checking for wet diapers and checking in
baby-proofing and proofing essays
wiping noses
and contemplating your next major work of prose
all this you do
while getting an unwilling captive to fall
asleep

add the leap into a long distance love affair
and what you have
is a seething cauldron of angst
without time any for brooding
mood swings

are for people with hours on end/to spend journaling
about longing
with days upon days to sit melancholy by a fucking window
doodling an absent lover's last name
in red
in bold/block letters
intertwined with curly-cues
with the backdrop of whispered *I love you*'s
and long luxurious sighs

my life is not the life of Emily Dickenson
nor am I a fucking Virginia Woolf
not only because I am Black/more because
I lack the idyllic tempo of their lives
as wives and childless daughters of rich white men

plus
my missing lover is three thousand miles removed
which is really a lifetime
when you are in the middle of a crisis
an eon
when you lack the resources
to hop from tarmac to train

whenever you find the moment to ache
there is always something pulling at you
at me
at us
I can barely find time
to reminisce
about the times we were actually together
I just have to trust the curve of history that connects us
remind myself that what separates us is land

our flesh may yearn/our feet flap with the desire
to click our heels red
but this love ain't no fairy tale

and we would be dead/without pulse
if we were to depend on Dorothy and her dog
Oz is just some well-told tale
of lions and missing hearts
with more courage than we have had for decades

it has been years of crossing borders
for these passions
money has always been thin ice
good thing New York/Chinese don't cost much
and caramel ice cream is still my cheap pleasure

in the moments when I indulge
when I dare to linger in a moment
quick with memories

I am once again in the house
in which we first made love
proper/like adults
even though we still smelled like children
we laughed loud/like we knew
what we were doing/would cost us

freedom and desire
distance and chains

proximity is what we get drunk on
these days/we move
with the weight of consequence in our reach
we hope mostly/for what is possible
limitless/in imagination
in actuality/we spend every morning together
electronic medium/while the child pulls
at cords
keys

screen-shots moving
wipes/teethers/toys that squeak

tweak the picture and we could be anywhere
together
in the same space

but this day don't leave much time for no dreaming

so off you go
call if you find a minute
send me a note/I'll be toting this kid
from bed to bath/my path littered
with snippets of what you said
all day
you'll be in my head
and before we know it/it will be

nighttime

I will think of you then
morning/evening
you might even be able to have me at lunch/one day
we might share more than these
snatches/of borrowed spaces

race with me now
from frenzy to familiar
bear with me
in the scheduled agony of the accepted
hope with me
that this harried routine of separate lives
will soon shift from this all too fathomable frustration
toward a more serendipitously settled end

ACKNOWLEDGMENTS

How does one acknowledge a lifetime of support from a village too expansive to list? Not one poem could have been written, much less published, without the global village that is my very lifeline.

My mother, Hazel, provided the most fantastically, sorcerously, witchy life upon which I've hung almost all my writing. When she was young, it was common knowledge that my mother was a teller of stories—stories everyone knew to be lies. Five decades later, these lies have become the truth of my life. She imagined my life—travel, profession, freedom—for herself. I am indeed, my mother's wildest dream come true, not for her, but for many others.

My late grandmother, Bernice Perry, gave me nine stable years of life to contrast with the unstable life my moving-target mother created. My grandmother stayed, even when given the chance of leaving us for a better life, for the United States; she chose to stay—in the poorest of conditions—with my brother and me. I do not have the words to write how much that steadies my pen.

My little sister Larah's survival of my mother parallels my own. I'm so proud of all you've done. Thanks for providing a picture of my mother in another time. Without you, I wouldn't have seen much of who she was/is. Thanks for being who you are, for being so frank about your own experience of her. It has helped me to be clearer about mine.

When I landed in America I had almost no one. I was undocumented and alone. More than once, I found myself without a home, staying with friends whenever there was a spare place to lay my head—but in this New York City, free space is never permanent. I've stayed on someone's couch in the NYC housing projects in Canarsie. I've spent nights in my friend's mother's bed when the mother in question went on vacation to Jamaica. For the first few years, home remained an elusive reality. Then entered Peter. Peter was my magical, fairy godfather who loved fashion and flounces and Kangol hats and who wrote poetry. He first became my friend, then my writing partner in crime. Then my partner, by law—it didn't matter that I was an lesbian, or that he was a gay man. To quote Peter, family can be a choice. So we made the choice to become family, to have and raise children together—in a world that truly has room for all the possibilities of identity and sexuality and ways of being. And by that I mean he married me and took me home to his mother Carole Linda. Without Peter Conti none of who I've become would have been possible. Peter died before the LGBTQIA community won the right to marry, so it was the strangest thing to find myself both a lesbian and a widow. In truth, I really couldn't complain, because Peter was gone, but he had bequeathed me an incredible group of humans, my in-laws who are not only my legal clan but also my tribe in spirit and in heart.

Chris Conti, the youngest brother of Peter Conti, is my brother-in-law. He's also one of the finest men I know. Peter died before we could get to the baby-making part of things, so Chris, in the most unselfish act of kindness, provided the necessary other half of my daughter's DNA. He's been the best of brothers to me. He remains my daughter's Baba and an unshakable pillar in my daughter's life. Everything I am can be traced back to the miracle of Peter and his family. I offer my heartfelt gratitude to the band of extraordinary human beings my late husband called family.

I've had many part-time, stand-in mothers, who made space for me in the families they created—without them, I wouldn't have known the beauty of kindness. Their presence spans the length of my life and stretches across countries. Carole Conti, my mother-in-law, is—in every way—a miracle. Carole Linda, each day I rise I count myself lucky that you were born, that you gave birth to the two men who have most deeply affected my adult life. Thank you for raising your children to be the kind of openhearted that borders on the insane. I gained so much when I married your son—a tribe to call my own, an entire family for my daughter, and a home in which I spent years by the sea making the kind of history of which legends are told. The greatest among these gifts is your friendship.

Big thank you to my Jamaican mothers: the late June Lewis, Elaine Wint-Leslie, Leilith Burnett, and Dorette Buchanan. To my African American activists, Mama Ruby Sales, who, along with her partner Cheryl Blankenship, adopted me as soon as they met me in my early twenties. And my biggest gratitude to Susan Barrow, who immediately opened her home and her heart to me, first because I was partnered to her daughter and second because we are kindred spirits.

So big hugs to Bamidele Adedoyin and Yako Prodis, my sister wife and brother husband. We've walked a long, beautiful trail together. We were friends before we were parents. We have suffered the gentrifiers and the subsequent fracturing of our communities caused by displacement from Brooklyn. We have many more philosophical conversations to have—many more sessions of truth and denial to process. These poems are only a few of the windows through which we have looked together. Here's to another twenty years of friendship and another cadre of poems to come.

For a person with so few ties to my biological family, I've been lucky to have the very best band of folks become my chosen family: Sandra Mullings, Lisa Mullings, Maziki Thame, Cynthia Randall, Annmarie Lawson, Vivette Miller, Racquel Bremmer, Gloria Bigelow, Leleti Russell, Angela Williams, Asha Lewis, Andrea Barrow, Shontina Vernon, Raquel Thompson, Keondra Freemyn, Patricia Thomas, Frances Goldin, Marcia Thurmond, Michelle Hampton, Orinthia Swindell, Lekshmi Cashmore, Zenzile Keith, Kelly Gillespie, Leigh-Ann Naidoo, Mwenya Kabwe, Mazuba Haanyama, Gifford Rankine, Greg Thames, Asif Williams, Trudy Belnavis, Aliya Leslie, Meshell Ndegeocello, Allison Riley, Cree Summer, Sekiya Dorsett, Dominique Christina Johnson, L. Vogel, Arlene Burnett, and Paul and Saskia Thompson. You litter the planet like stars in a clear night sky. Together, you form the map of a constellation that consistently guides me back to a self of which I can be proud. I love ya'll like cook-food. Thanks for listening to my self-indulgent musings on the meaning of our lives and for being witness to this litany of ungraceful survival.

I'm indebted to the writers and activists who have supported my work and always reminded me that humanity is a work in progress. Thank you, Walter Mosley, for always pushing me to write more, do more, try more avenues in the vein of telling stories. To Edwidge Danticat who continues to write stories I wish I had written.

To the writers who create/d work that made me think I was possible: June Jordan, Sonia Sanchez, Audre Lorde, Lorna Goodison, Jean "Binta" Breeze, Dorothy Allison, Dionne Brand, Alice Walker, your words keep me afloat. All day. Every day.

And my widest, warmest, most engulfing gratitude to Jacqueline Woodson, who right away said yes to writing a foreword for a book of poems with multiple themes spanning decades. Thank you for centering the Black experience in your work. Thank you for living a life which proves that hard work, a willingness to love who you choose, a commitment to raising Black children in Brooklyn, and not taking oneself too seriously, can be the ingredients for a successful writer's life. Your wicked-sharp wit, disguised as your sense of humor, remains one of my favorite things about you.

And my joy of joys, Zuri-Siale Chin, who arrived and upended my world, I owe you a trailer-load of gratitude. This journey with you has been the wildest, most beautiful of poems. You teach me so much about love. Thanks for showing me how to be both fierce and fearless while being extraordinarily kind. All you have taught me cannot be contained in these too-few pages. This poem we are writing is epic and filled with the sound of your laughter. Each verse is an unexpected joy. I love who you are—who you reveal yourself to be as you grow. I'm so looking forward to the days ahead. Here's hoping the many stanzas we have to yet write will surprise us and that the sadnesses we have yet to survive will only be a small weight when countered with the balance of our shared joy.

I am certain I have omitted the names of people who continue to love and support my work and life. Forgive me. These pages aren't infinite, and my memory is less than what it was. Know that as you read, I lie awake, inking your names into this incomplete list of the loves of my beautifully imperfect life.

ABOUT THE AUTHOR

Poet, actor, and performing artist Staceyann Chin is the author of the critically acclaimed memoir *The Other Side of Paradise*, cowriter and original performer in the Tony Award–winning *Russell Simmons Def Poetry Jam on Broadway*, and author of the one-woman shows *Hands Afire, Unspeakable Things, Border/Clash*, and *MotherStruck*. She has appeared on the *Oprah Winfrey Show* and *60 Minutes*, and her poetry been featured in the *New York Times* and *Washington Post*. She proudly identifies as Caribbean, Black, Asian, lesbian, a woman, and a resident of New York City, as well as a Jamaican national.

ABOUT HAYMARKET BOOKS.

Haymarket Books is a radical, independent, nonprofit book publisher based in Chicago.

Our mission is to publish books that contribute to struggles for social and economic justice. We strive to make our books a vibrant and organic part of social movements and the education and development of a critical, engaged, international left.

We take inspiration and courage from our namesakes, the Haymarket martyrs, who gave their lives fighting for a better world. Their 1886 struggle for the eight-hour day—which gave us May Day, the international workers' holiday—reminds workers around the world that ordinary people can organize and struggle for their own liberation. These struggles continue today across the globe—struggles against oppression, exploitation, poverty, and war.

Since our founding in 2001, Haymarket Books has published more than five hundred titles. Radically independent, we seek to drive a wedge into the risk-averse world of corporate book publishing. Our authors include Noam Chomsky, Arundhati Roy, Rebecca Solnit, Angela Y. Davis, Howard Zinn, Amy Goodman, Wallace Shawn, Mike Davis, Winona LaDuke, Ilan Pappé, Richard Wolff, Dave Zirin, Keeanga-Yamahtta Taylor, Nick Turse, Dahr Jamail, David Barsamian, Elizabeth Laird, Amira Hass, Mark Steel, Avi Lewis, Naomi Klein, and Neil Davidson. We are also the trade publishers of the acclaimed Historical Materialism Book Series and of Dispatch Books.